Creation, the Curse, and Culture

Woman's Journey Back to Wholeness, Dignity, and Significance

Donna L. McCormick

Altared Lives Ministries, Inc. provides holistic ministry to adults of all ages utilizing various methods including the World Wide Web, books, videos, music, and multimedia technology.

© 2015 Donna L. McCormick

All rights reserved. No part of this publication may be reproduced, stored in a retrieval system, or transmitted in any form without the express written consent of the publisher.

All Scripture references are from the New King James Version of the Holy Bible, Copyright 1982, Thomas Nelson, Inc., database © 2013 WORDsearch, unless otherwise noted. All rights reserved.

ISBN: 978-0-9787485-4-8

Cover design and layout by Donna L. McCormick

Published by Altared Lives Ministries, Inc.
P.O. Box 534
Hampton, VA 23669

Printed in the United States of America

CONTENTS

Preface   5

Introduction   9

Part I Creation: Common Purpose
1 Alone   13
2 Adequate   23
3 Advantageous   31
4 Advanced   35

Part II Curse: Common Problem
5 Punitive Situation   43
6 Perpetual Sensitivity   49
7 Presiding Superintendent   57

Part III Culture: Common Particularities
8 Layered Social Environment   65
9 Low Self-Esteem   77
10 Labyrinthine Spiraling Emotions   89

Part IV Christ: Crowning Perspective
11 Significant Verity   107
12 Supernatural Victory   123

Endnotes   139

Preface

I believe it was near 1996 when the kindling for this book ignited in my heart. I don't know what caused the embers to go out, since I am publishing my thoughts almost two decades later. But I recall what inspired me initially. I was sorely disappointed because a person I considered to be a close friend didn't really know me, or didn't want to know me, beyond a superficial level. When I expressed my disappointment over the friendship, however, the friend replied that perhaps we shouldn't be friends at all. I was absolutely crushed, because I had poured years of encouragement and caring into that friendship. And after the breach in fellowship, I considered myself to have no real friends. And that was a very lonely place to be, especially for a believer in Jesus Christ.

Shortly thereafter, a newly-ordained minister preached a sermonette at the church I attended. The sermonette resulted in a miracle leading to the healing process for my devastated emotions. At the end of her sermonette the minister asked the congregation to write on a scrap of paper the name of a big disappointment at that particular time in our lives. Then she had us come forward and toss the scrap of paper in a trash can, symbolizing that the trash is where we would leave it. I wrote down words that referred to my broken friendship. That friendship was representative of all my friendships, or lack thereof, throughout my life up until that time.

But a truly supernatural healing proceeded from that simple act of faith and obedience. I have no other explanation for it. I had been hurting for much of my life over a lack of meaningful friendships, and healing had finally materialized.

But it wasn't until my own emotional healing that I began to notice hurting women all around me. There were women hurting from various relationship sources: strained romances, painful marriages, issues with their children, and broken friendships. But there were two common threads linking all of those hurts:

> (1) The ladies all seemed to be struggling to receive complete healing, although they were members of what we called "Word churches" pastored by anointed teachers of the Bible; and,

> (2) Few of the pastors were addressing the emotional hurts with an understanding of the complexities of the female experience.

Because of extreme shyness and low self-esteem during my youth, I oftentimes had searched for resources that provided answers to my own loneliness and brokenness. I found precious little in the way of assistance, however. I searched for materials dealing with the psychological and emotional differences between males and females, seeking remedy for my loneliness. However, I found nothing that was useful and I remained in a state of pain for many years.

I had experienced numerous exhortations from male pastors urging women to "get out of your emotions" or "get over your emotions." Those admonitions seemed to be misguided (at best) to me, since men and women differ physiologically, hormonally, psychologically, and culturally. This results in the emotional constitution of females being measurably different from males in society, in general.

When I heard statements like "get out of your emotions" coming from our pastors, I would think, *they're telling us to get over something that God designed in us.* It's akin to someone telling men to get over their sex drive. How misguided would that be? Very misguided, because men are physiologically *designed* with the propensity to have a strong sex drive. The agent is called *testosterone*. It's a hormonal reality. Men are designed with it.

I don't know what happens at men's Christian retreats. But if/when they discuss sexual temptation or pornography, I would almost guarantee that a minister or counselor would not admonish them to simply "get over your sex drive," and leave it at that. Leaders would more than likely provide strategies or instruction on how to avoid temptation. Or I presume they might teach about how to deal with a fall into sexual sin. The men wouldn't simply be exhorted to get over a weakness that could destroy them or adversely affect their relationship with God and their families.

So God doesn't expect women to simply "get over" our emotions any more than He expects men to get over their sex drive. Women are physiologically designed to experience diverse emotions more intensely than men. It's a hormonal reality.

What God desires, however, is for us to express our emotions within boundaries that are godly, acceptable, and spiritually healthy – similar to His expectation of men to express their sex drive within boundaries that are godly, acceptable, and spiritually healthy. Doesn't that sound more sensible?

I've written *Creation, the Curse, and Culture* to help hurting or confused women to find their way back to wholeness, dignity, and significance. God's design, the results of the fall of man, and our cultural environment all have a defining impact on us as women. Creation, the curse, and culture have directed and impacted *woman's* journey in life from the foundation of her existence until now.

As an aside, I use the term "woman" in parentheses and italics at various points in this book. Those formatted usages represent the embodiment of God's creation of woman as He envisioned and created her to be. So when you come across "woman" or *woman* in this book, envision God's ideal and intended creation of *woman* that embodies all of us. Think of Eve prior to the fall – that's who "woman" was supposed to be, expressed in all the diversity of women today.

What, why, and *how* we are as women proceed from creation, first and foremost, then from the curse and the culture in which we now live. Multitudes of hurting women have not experienced complete healing because few seeking to help women have effectively incorporated an awareness of creation, the curse, and culture in ministering to us. Creation, the curse, and culture are determinant realities that shape who we are.

In our journey back to wholeness, dignity, and significance from brokenness, we cannot neglect any of the three spheres of reality in ministry to women. All three – creation, the curse, and culture – are major contributors to our sense of fulfillment as women. So unless those factors are brought into perspective in ministry to hurting women, we will be shortchanged in finding lasting, in-depth solutions that bring restoration to our souls.

Introduction

Emotional upheavals. Unfulfilling romance cycles. Self-esteem struggles. Depression. Eating disorders. Uncontested physical abuse.

Debilitating challenges plague many in our society. However, issues such as these are far more prevalent among females than among males. These conditions are more characteristic of the female experience than the male experience. But whatever the incidence, the issues are unquestionably unhealthy, unwanted, and sometimes unresolved, even among Christians.

But who has the solutions? And why haven't we seen large-scale movement toward healing? And why do we see the same issues transcending race, class, and religion?

That's what this book investigates. Many books have been written about the topic. Many sermons have been delivered on the subject. Countless solutions have been proposed. And yet, we continue to see these same issues among women – even among believers. It's understandable that the healing we have access to, according to the Bible, is absent among those who reject (or simply are unaware of) the tenets of faith that we hold dear. For example, when the Bible says, "He restores my soul…" (Psalm 23:3), it's understandable that an atheist would be less prone to believe or acknowledge such an experience from a God in Whom he does not believe.

But for those who know, love, and serve God, it's difficult to explain why we experience the unrest and disheveled lives that we do for years on end.

Or is it as difficult to explain as it seems to be?

Our relationship with our Lord was designed to be one of continual growth and discovery of Him and of ourselves. So pitfalls and hurts will inevitably blindside us on occasion because we're never going to be perfectly mature on this side of heaven. But to experience the same hurts, challenges, and upheavals time and time again, year after year, decade after decade, is certainly not His desire for us – nor is it reflective of His design.

With this book, I desire to crack open the case for why we, as women, are the way we are, and why we experience the things we do. Ultimately, the goal is to share how we can be healed and regain the wholeness and esteem that God originally intended. But such a realization involves recognition of some conditions that are a result of creation, what happened after the fall of man ("the curse"), and the role culture plays in our struggles.

Ultimately, the way we overcome our issues is between God and us. But if we understand more about ourselves, and are honest with ourselves and with God, I believe we can foster improvement in how our lives transpire.

Some of our challenges will not change until Jesus returns. However, some conditions can be improved before that point in time. Some solutions will need to be supported by significant others. And by "significant others," I do not mean spouses, necessarily. I'm referring to anyone that might have a great deal of influence or input into our lives, including children, parents, and friends. However, God placed within us an inherent resiliency, if we can tap into it. We can still be made whole by His power in the midst of disorder. And the specific path to *that* healing and wholeness lies within us, despite what others around us do or don't do concerning us.

But I will caution you that this won't be easy. Improvement in anything that's worthwhile takes much effort. And no improvement can come without change.

Half of the battle is realizing that something is *wrong*. The next twenty-five percent is realizing that something *absolutely has to change* – whether it is within us, or around us. And the final twenty-five percent involves *committing* to the change.

Of course, the percentages I've given are arbitrary and subjective. We certainly can control – or more accurately, *influence* – more than twenty-five percent of what happens in our lives. Someone once said that life's outcomes consist of ten percent of what happens to us, and ninety percent of how we *respond* to what happens to us. The important thing to realize, then, is that we are most accountable for our responses. They impact our lives the most.

That being said, I do not claim to possess the magic slingshot to slay all of your emotional giants. Yet I hope what you encounter in the remainder of this book will help you to begin to ask the right questions that bring you to wholeness. I'm hopeful that what I share will enable you to pick up five smooth stones and run toward the proverbial giants that are robbing you of peace and joy. If we determine where we stand, where we are headed, and what our obstacles are, we have a fighting chance of making progress.

However, let me add that this book has not been written to make you feel good. I hope that you will feel good when you see the value that God places upon your life. But my aim is not to make you feel good. It's not important to me that you feel *good*. It's vitally important that you feel *God*.

In today's slang, to "feel" another is to understand that person's point of view. It means to comprehend another person's perspective. To feel someone means to see things from inside another's head, or to look at things from behind the windows of another's eyes.

I want you to feel God. You need to feel God to understand what it means to be a woman. You need to feel God to understand how to capitalize on the uniqueness of the female experience. You need to feel God to develop healthier ways of responding to emotional challenges as His unique creation of "woman." You need to feel God to diminish the anguish of the curse. You need to feel God to subvert the dysfunctional trappings of our culture.

So don't be focused on a "feel good" message. Focus on comprehending God's message to you through this book.

Are you ready for your journey back to wholeness, dignity, and significance? I hope so, because we're about to go looking for those stones to slay some giants. Let's run to the battle!

Part I *Creation: Common Purpose*
1 Alone

Genesis 2:18
And the LORD God said, "It is not good that man should be alone; I will make him a helper comparable to him."

It might be a bit puzzling to you that I titled this chapter "Alone" when the opening Scripture is about man *not* being alone. I wanted to illustrate a poignant antithesis. The contrast between *alone* and God's discussion of man *not* being alone might call to mind a fear of isolation versus emotional security that is found in companionship. The juxtaposition of "alone" and *not* being alone might paint a picture of a seemingly never-ending chapter of singleness versus a promise of togetherness with a special person. Perhaps the divergence of the opposing concepts brings to mind disappointing realities of divorce versus childhood expectations of being married "forever."

Being alone is a stark reality for many of us. But God's intention from antiquity was for man *not* to be alone. God said it was not good for man to be alone.

This is not to cast a dark shadow over the state of relationships today. I simply want to bring attention to the fact that failed relationships have caused a great deal of pain in the lives of average people, including Christians. Certainly not every relationship has been unsuccessful. But many have, and to ignore that fact would not do justice to the people whose lives God desires to improve.

I'm a firm believer that to get to the bottom of any issue, you have to look at its origin. Therefore, in order to find the answers that bring women to wholeness, we must first consider our origin to determine who *woman* is, how she was designed, and why she came into existence. The answers to those three questions – who she is, how she came to be who she is, and why she exists – are first and foremost addressed by looking at creation. Therefore God's perspective is where we need to start when seeking to restore wholeness, dignity, and significance to women.

I shared my testimony about supernatural deliverance from emotional hurt in the preface. The hurt from which I was healed was deep emotional pain from a friend's taking our friendship much more lightly than I had. Please understand that my hurt was not a romantic heartbreak. The friend happened to be male, but we were not romantically involved. My deep heartache came from the fact that we had been friends for several years. And this friend – the only friend I felt that I had at the time – did not consider our friendship worth salvaging. So after the departure, I felt very *alone*. We were created for relationships, and I was alone. In fact, I had been alone – without true friends – for most of my life (childhood, included).

That was not God's design or desire for me. It's not His will for anyone to be isolated and alone. His desire and design is for healthy relationships to flourish in our lives.

Our entire universe revolves around *relationships*. There are relationships between planets and stars. There are relationships between geography and climate.

There are relationships between foods and nourishment. There are relationships between predators and their prey. Relationships such as these shape the environment.

Likewise, there are relationships that govern the dynamics of our natural lives. But I'm not just talking about human relationships, although those are critical and part of the big picture. There are relationships that govern the dynamics of how we act and react, how we think, and how we assess our surroundings, for instance. There are relationships between our philosophy of life and our general outlook on life. There are relationships between self-improvement plans and the outcomes of their implementation. There are relationships between our perceptions and our commitment to change circumstances in our lives.

What transpires in our heads, hearts, and natural surroundings dictates circumstances in our lives. We must realize these truths if we want to change certain aspects of our lives. We act according to our belief systems and perceptions. The more knowledgeable we are about interactions between thoughts, beliefs, and environment, the better equipped we will be to take advantage of opportunities to improve ourselves and thus, our lives.

If we want to experience better relationships in our lives, we have to develop more self-awareness. We absolutely have to know more about ourselves. Part of that awareness revolves around God's original design and purpose for us as women. Through acknowledgment of God's plan at the outset, we can begin to amass understanding. Then we can devise strategies to improve our lives in the area of our relationships. If we commit to taking action based upon progressive self-awareness, it changes our perceptions, and the quality of our relationships can improve substantially.

But first things first. This book might not be for you if you believe that we evolved from something less than human. In other words, if you believe that there was no divine hand in creating us, what I have to say may not appeal to you. As women, who we are, how we are, and why we exist originates with our Creator. God's thought process resulted in His assessment that man should not be alone. God saw that man should not seek to conquer his natural surroundings by himself. God surmised that man should not take on his daily tasks as a solitary soul. So God decided to remedy the predicament of "aloneness" that the man faced by creating "woman."

This brings us full circle to the subject "alone" once more, and the opening Scripture. There is a common purpose associated with why woman was originally created. Let's look at our reference Scripture again:

> *And the Lord God said, "It is not good that man should be alone; I will make him a helper comparable to him."*
>
> *Genesis 2:18*

That's our common purpose, ladies. If we begin with this, we can conclude that the remedy to emotional and relational struggles can be formulated from God's common purpose for us. Despite other factors that have distorted our perceptions of who we are, how we are, and why we exist, answers to our relationship dilemmas ultimately proceed from the One Who created us in the first place. Answers proceed from the purpose of our original Designer. Genesis 2:18 is the foundation of our inherent value.

An analogy that illustrates this is as follows. Let's say that you own a BMW automobile. All of a sudden one day, you hear a rattling sound coming from the engine. Would you take the car to a Schwinn bicycle shop to have the issue diagnosed and repaired? I certainly hope you would not do that! That would not make sense. Furthermore, the shop attendants would think that you had lost your mind if you entertained the expectation that a bicycle technician could repair your BMW!

So do you see how critical it is to go back to God, first and foremost, for our relationship and emotional challenges? If I can convince you to commit to assessing perceptions about yourself primarily from God's perspective, this book will have served its purpose. Because He designed us, we can utilize His maintenance and repair book (the Bible) to break chains that lock us in recurring patterns of emotional disappointment and dysfunction.

So let's look at the opening Scripture more closely. The Lord said that it was not good for man to be alone. Given that woman was created so that man would not be alone (our common purpose), it would not make sense for woman – or anyone – to then feel alone in God's world, do you agree? Terms that mean the same thing as *alone* include companionless, by oneself, isolated, or unaccompanied. So God stated that it was not good for man to be companionless, by himself, isolated, or unaccompanied – "alone."

Let me make an interesting point here: God did not bring Eve immediately on the scene for Adam when He said that it wasn't good for man to be alone. We see from the Scriptures that God first brought the animals to Adam, so that Adam could name them. In the very next verses after Genesis 2:18 in which God proclaimed that it was not good for man to be alone (and that He'd make a suitable helper for the man), we see the following in verses nineteen and twenty:

> [19] *Out of the ground the LORD God formed every beast of the field and every bird of the air, and brought them to Adam to see what he would call them. And whatever Adam called each living creature, that was its name.*
>
> [20] *So Adam gave names to all cattle, to the birds of the air, and to every beast of the field. But for Adam there was not found a helper comparable to him.*
>
> Genesis 2:19-20

So God said that it wasn't good for man to be alone, and that He'd make a helper suitable for him. But then in the very next verse, we see that God brought the animals to Adam to see what Adam would call them.

This is critical. Please note that God charged *Adam* with naming the animals to see what he would call them. But let us recognize the following:

> *First*, God Himself was not trying to determine which creature would make a comparable helper for Adam. God is omniscient and already knew. God wanted *Adam* to name the animals and recognize his *own* lack of a suitable helper.
>
> *Second*, Adam did not call even *one* of the animals a name indicative of his recognition that *any* of them constituted an appropriate helper or companion for himself.

The two observations above are key. Keep in mind that it was Adam – not God – who needed to recognize that an appropriate helper was not in the ranks of the animals. We will see why this is so important in another chapter.

But let's turn the spotlight on the term "alone" once more. God declared that it was not good for man to be alone. But many of us ("women") *are* alone. We should not fail to acknowledge at this juncture that it is partly due to *our* being alone – with the stigma or unpleasant realities surrounding such a condition – that many women enter into destructive patterns of behavior, or enter into ill-advised relationships.

The compelling factor for God was to provide woman for man so that *man* would not be alone. But in our time, the driving factor for many women entering into relationships is for *us* not to be alone. God said man shouldn't be alone, but individual women say, "No, it's *me* that shouldn't be alone."

Do you find that to be ironic? I do. I am not trying to start a weird doctrine or anything of the sort. Let's just take this at face value: God said that man shouldn't be alone; that it was not good for him. But today, we (women) say it's not good for *us* be alone.

Would you like to discover what turned the tables and produced that feeling of deficiency in women? Or better still, perhaps we should ask what is a beneficial way to address that attitude (especially since it is usually women who, by-and-large, feel so alone prior to having men in our lives).

Even if what remains in the pages of this book does not fully satisfy your longing and curiosity, I hope that you will at least gain additional understanding of yourself. A greater understanding of yourself will go a long way to restoring wholeness, dignity, and significance to your life.

But here's a disclaimer: I am one of those people who doesn't believe that I have to have all the answers to everything. Having all the answers is God's job – not mine. Believers walk by faith, *not* having all the answers.

I've discovered that a better activity than trying to have all the answers is asking enough of the right questions. That's how a scientist goes about her job. People have the misconception that scientists have all the answers. I function as a scientist in the secular arena and I assure you, scientists don't have all the answers. We ask all the questions. And eventually, we stumble across an answer. But we ask a lot of questions to get one answer.

And that's what I hope to accomplish as we delve into the effects of creation, the curse, and culture upon women. I don't have all the answers for the complexities of life. However, I hope that I can teach you to ask the right questions. And in so doing, perhaps you will discover the one answer that you need in order to live the most fulfilling life that God purposed for you.

Finally, please understand that I am not saying that you have to have a husband or a man in your life to be in God's perfect plan, or to have a fulfilling life. I'm not saying that at all. The common purpose for us was so that man wouldn't be alone. But God does not lock us into one option for a fulfilling life – marriage versus the "misery" of being alone. There are plenty of single Christians who are perfectly satisfied being single – I have been one of them the majority of my life.

I'm simply acknowledging the fact that most women desire some kind of companionship at *some* point in their lives, even if they have remained single all of their lives. There is probably at least one period of life during which most of us have considered dating or marriage. And let's face it – if we want to build a family God's way, His plan involves marriage before childbearing.

There is nothing wrong with desiring a mate. There is also nothing wrong with not desiring a mate. But we need to be emotionally healthy for either state we choose to pursue.

However, if we desire healthy relationships, no matter what types they are – romantic, familial, or platonic – we need to acknowledge that truly being alone is not God's best for *anyone* – man or woman.

Part I *Creation: Common Purpose*
2 Adequate

Genesis 2:18
And the LORD God said, "It is not good that man should be alone; I will make him a helper comparable to him."

Now that the topsoil of common purpose is out of the way, let's begin to dig deeper into the rich ground where all the nutrients are for our restoration. As you can see, Genesis 2:18 is our reference Scripture again. You will also notice that this chapter is titled, "Adequate." That word is what I want you to focus on – adequate. *Adequate.* Spell it:

A-D-E-Q-U-A-T-E

Adequate!

Genesis 2:18 states that God purposed to make a helper comparable to Adam. Comparable has the meaning of suitable, fit, appropriate, properly befitting, synergistic, similar, and complementary. I summed all those words up into one: *adequate.* Woman is an adequate helper for man.

Let's liken it to a large picture puzzle that only has two pieces. The pieces are not mirror images – they are complementary. Where one has a jagged edge, the other has a jagged recess. Where one piece has a downward slant to the right, the other piece has an incline to the left. Where one has a unique geometrical configuration, the other has a matching void, in contrast. I'm not trying to be sensual, so if your mind went there, please come back. We're talking about two puzzle pieces. One is complementary to the other piece. It is *adequate* to fit harmoniously together to form the entire beautiful picture. However, there is a frame for the two-piece puzzle, and an environment in which the puzzle pieces exist.

Maybe the picture puzzle is lying on a coffee table. Maybe it is lying on the kitchen table. Maybe it is hanging on the wall. Maybe it is in the attic. It has its own frame, and its own environment. It is wherever it is, for its own purpose. Keep this in mind as we go further.

Please allow me to take a little creative liberty. We don't know what language Adam spoke, but let me simulate the dialogue in English, since that's what we speak.

So when God created Adam, God brought all His other creations to Adam for Adam to name them. Adam took on the task nobly, and with vigor, because he was obedient and apparently valued his relationship with God and the animals. We can presume that Adam was diligent because he completed the task, according to Genesis chapter two and verse twenty,

> *"So Adam gave names to all cattle, to the birds of the air, and to every beast of the field..."*
> *Genesis 2:20a*

Now let's liken the animals to puzzle pieces in God's great panorama for His creation. Adam looked at all the other puzzle pieces and said, "You are 'bird' and you fit in the air and the trees. You are 'bear' and you fit over there in the forest. You are 'mole' and you fit in the soil.

You are 'frog' and you fit in the marshes," and so on. But Adam never said, "You are (fill in the blank) and you belong here beside me!"

He did not tell the cockatoo that. He did not tell the baboon that. He did not tell the mouse that. He did not tell the horse, the dog, or the cat that. He did not tell any of them that. Adam realized he didn't have a puzzle piece in creation comparable to *him*. He finished his assignment of naming the animals and the Scripture says,

> *"But for Adam there was not found a helper comparable to him."*
>
> Genesis 2:20b

That was primarily the reason God had Adam name all the creatures around him. Adam needed to find a comparable or adequate helper. However, he did not find one. Can you imagine a perfect specimen of a man, with big innocent eyes, diligently looking for a helper comparable to him, yet not finding one?

God knew Adam's helper had to be very special to him. And ultimately, Adam came to the same conclusion by default. There was none among the puzzle pieces of creation that was *adequate* to be Adam's helper in the environment God had prepared for him.

What you can gather from this is the fact that you will be adequate for the man who is right for you. You will be adequate for the friends that were meant for you. Now, this does not mean that you won't have areas where you can improve – you will, and so will the man and any friends. We all do. And all of us should strive to improve in those areas. But you will be adequate for, and comparable to, the man who is right for you and for the friends that are right for you. You will be a suitable, comparable, complementary helper for the man, and suitable, comparable, or complementary for the friends that are meant to be in your life.

This is key, because Proverbs chapter thirty-one and verse ten is taught incorrectly in some circles as it concerns a man and his mate. I was taught, and maybe some of you were, too, that the virtuous woman is a rare find. But that's not what the Scripture says. I switch to King James Version now, because it correctly translates the original Hebrew word into the same English word in verse ten as it does later in the passage. That's important in order to gain a correct interpretation. Proverbs 31:10 asks:

> Who can find a **virtuous** woman? For her price is far above rubies.
> Proverbs 31:10 KJV

Verse ten simply asks a question, and then states the value of the virtuous woman as being far above rubies. The Scripture does not intimate that she is rare – it states that she is very *valuable*.

We know she's not rare because in verse 29 of the same chapter, the same word is used when the Bible says,

> Many daughters have done **virtuously**, but thou excellest them all.
> Proverbs 31:29 KJV

Did you see that? It says, "Many daughters have done virtuously ..." *Many* have done virtuously. The word "virtuously" in verse twenty-nine is the same Hebrew word in verse ten for "virtuous" where the writer asks,

"Who can find a *virtuous* woman?" It is translated into English as the same word in most translations.

Many, the Scripture says. *Many* have done virtuously. Many does not denote something that is rare.

If I say that I have many ideas, it means my ideas are plentiful. If I say that there are many trees in my yard, it means there are numerous trees in my yard.

So receive in your heart that there are many virtuous women, and you could very well be one of them. If so, your value is above that of precious gems. That is really what verse ten says.

If we look at other translations, and consider the context of the passage, we will see that the speaker or writer is not talking to a woman at all. The discourse is directed to a *man*, Lemuel. In other words, the primary emphasis is not on the virtuous woman. The focus is upon who can recognize her and what constitutes her value.

The speaker extols the characteristics of that type of woman in verses ten to twenty-nine, so that the *man* who is being taught can *recognize* her. (Flashback now to Adam's realization that a suitable helper for him was not found among the animals.) Near the end of the discourse in Proverbs, the speaker tells the man (Lemuel) that charm is deceitful, and beauty is temporary, but that a woman who reverences the Lord shall be praised. That's a virtuous woman.

But look at Proverbs 31:29 again. At that point, the conversation is directed to the virtuous woman about whom the speaker is talking. The speaker states,

Many daughters have done virtuously, but thou excellest them all.
Proverbs 31:29 KJV

She outshines all the other virtuous women, in the opinion of the *speaker* or *writer* – for whatever reason(s) he deems befitting.

Did you catch that?

That's crucial. Let's return to our original discussion about Adam. Adam saw that there was not a helper that was comparable to him, that complemented him, or that was suitable for him. Adam needed a complementary helper that was adequate for and well-suited to *him*. He came to the realization that there was none like that in his environment. And that's good, because there really wasn't a choice that even remotely was adequate for him in the animal kingdom. But Adam had to recognize that for *himself*. God put His man in a situation where the man had the opportunity to come to that conclusion for himself, and Adam passed with flying colors.

But during the time of the Proverbs discourse, as it is today, there were and are other *adequate* women. There were other virtuous women in the environment of the speaker in Proverbs chapter thirty-one, as there are other virtuous women today. But in Proverbs, the speaker saw something special in his woman, for his personal situation, for his own complementary puzzle piece. And that's the way it should be today.

Today's challenge is that, unlike Adam or the man in Proverbs chapter thirty-one, some men do not know what is adequate for them. They do not know how to locate her or to decide who is adequate for them. I'm talking about Christian men. Many choose by worldly standards (beauty, libido, and so on).

For whatever reason(s), these men do not choose to remain single. The result has been the decision to marry anyway, getting hurt, and/or emotionally damaging the choice of a wife when things don't work out because she was not the *adequate* choice for him. Or both injured parties become scarred emotionally when they are not willing to commit to working out difficulties within the marriage. Likewise, some women do not know for whom they are adequate.

So because of the insufficiency of the dating process and its warped dynamics (the world's mentality), people potentially end up in numerous relationships where many individuals are wounded in repeated cycles of dysfunction. The final result is that the divorce rate continues to climb. Or people engage in extramarital affairs. Or individuals who *aren't* single wish that they *were*, while some that are still single wish they were not single. I'm talking about Christians.

Thus the original plan of God – that is, for the man to realize his specific complementary puzzle piece is missing – is obscured by the myriad of contexts today in which we foster relationships. Today both the man and the woman have neglected to allow God to lead them to the correct realization of their *adequate* mate.

Adequate does not equate to an "I'll settle" type of attitude. It's not a "this will do – it's adequate for my needs" mentality. No, no, no. Our definition of adequate in God's context means *comparable, befitting, suitable,* and *complementary* – what Eve was for Adam. We're not discussing a "consolation prize" or a "this-will-do-in-my-heat-of-the-moment" type of relationship.

When God brought Eve to Adam, He did not have to convince Adam to claim her! God did not have to coerce Adam or beat him over the head. Adam readily claimed her with the statement, *"This is now bone of my bones and flesh of my flesh; she shall be called Woman, because she was taken out of Man"* (Genesis 2:23).

The conclusion of the matter is that you will be adequate for those with whom you're comparable, especially a romantic interest. He will recognize it, and so will you. You have been designed to be adequate. Cease from belittling yourself by thinking that you are inadequate. And God forbid any of you seeking to coerce or convince someone into being with you, by any means!

Will he, or you, be "perfect"? Of course not – none of us are, male or female. We all have areas in which we need to improve. But adequate, yes – you most certainly are adequate for the right man and the right friends.

It's akin to the lyric of a currently popular song where the male vocalist confesses to be infatuated with all of his lady's "perfect imperfections." That is a beautiful notion – her imperfections are perfect for him, in his estimation. Yes, you will be suitable, complementary, and comparable – or simply, "adequate" – for the right man.

Part I *Creation: Common Purpose*
3 Advantageous

Genesis 2:18
And the LORD God said, "It is not good that man should be alone; I will make him a helper comparable to him."

One last time, I begin with the Scripture we've been studying for the first two chapters. For this chapter, I want to highlight another word in the verse: *helper*. Recall that we are studying the "creation" facet of who we are, how we are, and why we exist, as women. We still are looking at God's common purpose for "woman."

I love the fact that God saw that the man needed a helper, and that woman was created to meet that need. The term *helper* signifies that there is an activity or assignment that the woman was created to assist the man in doing. This means that she held a special importance in God's scheme of things. Therefore we can deduce that her existence is *advantageous* to the man. There is a benefit in having her that man did not have before she was created.

This also signifies that she was not to be idle, or someone just for the man to gawk at or to marginalize – a trophy girl, if you will. The woman was to have something of substance to offer in the relationship she shared with the man. There was a common goal, a mutual assignment, or a joint task that they were to accomplish together. In this sense, her existence is for the *advantage* of the man. It was advantageous for him to have her in his life.

It is a compliment for God to have given woman such an esteemed position from the beginning. It is also a great responsibility. Realization of these two important facts – that it is an honor as well as a tremendous responsibility for God to have placed woman in man's life – leads to two conclusions:

> (1) Each man who seeks a helper needs a revelation and understanding concerning his assignment from God. He must be inclined to accomplish the assignment, otherwise he does not need a helper; and,

> (2) Each woman has to have a revelation that she is to assist man in God's task for the two of them in the earth.

These pivotal realizations for us as women should help us to see ourselves living a life of purpose rather than one of insignificance. This is not to say that women have no purpose unless we are a partner in what a man is doing. Not at all. Otherwise we that are single would become insignificant by default, and that is the opposite of what this book is all about – significance because of God's design.

I simply want to show the wonderful plan of God, in giving *woman* a place right beside man in fulfilling God's purposes in the earth. I am conveying the sheer magnificence of *woman* in God's original design and plan for her. She holds a special role in completing His intentions in the earth. And even if she doesn't have a special man in her life, she can still assist man in general, in God's common purpose for her to be a helper. She can accomplish tasks in society-at-large as well as in the house of God that fulfill God's purpose in her being advantageous to man.

Some women feel unimportant and insignificant, particularly if they *don't* have a man by their side or if they haven't brought children into the world. But God's intention was for *woman* to share in the significant role He developed for man in the earth. That hasn't changed. Even though the earth and mankind have changed drastically from the days of the Garden of Eden, God's plan for man has not changed. God said,

> *So shall My word be that goes forth from My mouth; it shall not return to Me void, but it shall accomplish what I please, and it shall prosper in the thing for which I sent it.*
> *Isaiah 55:11*

So, what was the word that went forth from God's mouth concerning man and woman? What was His plan for them in the earth? We find it in the first chapter of Genesis:

> *Then God blessed them, and God said to them, "Be fruitful and multiply; fill the earth and subdue it; have dominion over the fish of the sea, over the birds of the air, and over every living thing that moves on the earth."*
> *Genesis 1:28*

So for anyone to relegate *woman* to just the function of childbearing and taking care of the home is a concept that is not supported per God's original plan. Those are two very important portions of the plan, no doubt. But

God's complete purpose for man and woman has never changed. In a nutshell, that purpose was to fill and *rule the earth*. Creation set His original plan in motion. Sin did not change His original plan. The curse did not change His original plan. Culture has not changed God's original plan.

Yes, we have a role in procreation. But so does the man. The man is not relegated to that responsibility alone, and neither is the woman. *Woman* was a significant facet of God's creation, and she still is. *Woman* was created and fashioned to be advantageous to the full purpose of God, alongside man, in the earth.

We still are. Whether married or not, or whether having procreated or not – *woman* is significant because of her design and God's plan for her from the beginning.

Our significance and dignity are not diminished by our marital condition or motherhood status. Our role in the earth is advantageous to mankind. God called us a helper. That's what He designed. That's what we are. Bank on it.

Part I *Creation: Common Purpose*
4 Advanced

Genesis 2:21-22
21And the LORD God caused a deep sleep to fall on Adam, and he slept; and He took one of his ribs, and closed up the flesh in its place. 22Then the rib which the LORD God had taken from man He made into a woman, and He brought her to the man.

Now we look at the last meaty morsel related to the creation of woman – the fact that she is *advanced*. Yes, advanced. It relates to woman's common purpose. The dictionary's most appropriate definition for our use of the word "advanced" is *ahead or far or further along in progress, complexity, knowledge, skill, etc.*[1]

This chapter's reference verses tell us that God fashioned woman from a rib of man. In other words, she was made from something that already had the life of God in it – "man." She was not made from dirt or clay like the man was. She was formed from what the Bible calls "a living soul" – what man became after God breathed into him (Genesis 2:7). Therefore, God started with more advanced "stuff" to make woman.

The fact that He made her from man holds significance for who she is because of the initial connection to the man. She came out of him, therefore she is like him. But she is different from him, also. I repeat, she is the same as the man, but at the same time, *not* the same as the man.

Let that sink in, because much of the time these days, women are fighting to be on the same level of existence as men. There are young ladies competing in the same sports alongside their male teammates. There are ladies competing in the same corporate environments as men. There are countless "how-to" books that coach women to think or act like men in various situations in order to be successful. The debate rages over being equal versus being the same. Are we the same? Are we equal? What do we have to give up, become, lose, gain, learn, or unlearn, to obtain equality, and to be seen as being on par with men?

These are integral questions that surface and resurface throughout our lives. And as we will see in part II and part III of this book, such considerations impact facets of who we are, how we are, and why we exist. These are not simply considerations that we as females must grasp and reconcile for ourselves. We must help men to understand them as well.

Our culture perpetuates an attitude about women that is very natural and accepted by both men and women. Although some people, for conscience's sake, might want to deny that such an attitude exists, the attitude is that a woman's most salient value is initially and primarily found in her physical attributes. This attitude sets the stage for overemphasis of a woman's attractiveness as opposed to valuing the intrinsic essence of who she is or what she represents. It causes us to focus on superficial embellishment in order to appear more attractive or alluring to men. However, that attitude detracts from our best emotional and psychological health as women. It detracts from our complete value in God's scheme of things, as well as in life, generally speaking.

There is an obsession in our culture with physical attractiveness. Revenue for the cosmetic industry alone in the United States is expected to exceed $62.5 billion in 2016.[2] But I will reserve further discussion of this topic for a subsequent chapter.

Please allow me to again reiterate that we are the result of creation, the curse, and culture. And all three affect our functioning in the various roles in which we find ourselves as women. However, *woman* was not designed to compete with man, but to complement him.

Don't get me wrong. There is nothing wrong with aspiring to non-traditional roles as women. Our adeptness in non-traditional roles basically is a testament to our efficacious design by God. The traditions of culture are what relegate us to roles that detract from our thorough design.

But there is a reason we were designed by God the way we are. We were not purposed by God to replace men. There is a reason we are more delicate physically. There is a reason our muscles have less physical mass than a man's muscles. There is a reason why our brains are wired differently from the man's brain. There is a reason we generally are smaller-framed than men, and weigh less than a man of similar height and body type.

We are advanced – for a reason. Remember that. Do not allow that fact to be diminished or underestimated. The things that are considered our weaknesses are actually the strengths that God designed into the blueprint of *woman*. We need to adjust our self-awareness about who we are and how we are designed. Then we can impact the perception that others have about us as females. We must educate ourselves, then educate others.

I know someone who believes that the more valuable an item is, the more abuse it should be able to take. But that is generally opposite of fact. The more valuable and advanced something is, the more complex it usually is. Thus it should be treated more delicately, not less. An expensive luxury car, for example, is usually not driven like a 1997 pickup truck over hill-and-dale in muddy terrain. Fine, tailored suits usually are not stuffed in the laundry basket and washed with denim jeans. Expensive electronics should not be thrown about or carelessly dropped on the sidewalk or in the pool. No, fine things are treated with more care, and even pampered, in some instances.

My brother taught me how to wash and wax my car so that I wouldn't damage the painted surface with swirl marks. He told me how often to have the oil changed, so I wouldn't damage the engine.

How much more consideration should "woman" receive? How much more should she be esteemed and respectfully treated?

This is not to diminish man's value one iota. It's to raise *woman's* value to the place where God purposed. *Woman* is *advanced*. God designed us differently from the way he designed every other living thing. He fashioned us from a creation that already carried His breath of life inside. He created us from a delicate structure obtained from within His most prized creation, man. God made woman from a living, breathing being! No other creation was made in this fashion.

Woman is advanced, emanating from God's specific intent to fashion her that way. Think about that, seriously. See to it that you never again diminish your worth, or allow anyone else to do so. Our design is marvelous and magnificent!

Please be reminded of my declaration in a previous chapter. My intent is not to make you feel good, but to make you feel God – to understand His perspective of you as "woman." So as a final discussion of this matter, let's consider a passage from the New Testament:

> ⁷*For a man indeed ought not to cover his head, since he is the image and glory of God; but woman is the glory of man.*
>
> ⁸*For man is not from woman, but woman from man.*
>
> ⁹*Nor was man created for the woman, but woman for the man.*
>
> ¹¹*Nevertheless, neither is man independent of woman, nor woman independent of man, in the Lord.*
>
> ¹²*For as woman came from man, even so man also comes through woman; but all things are from God.*
>
> 1 Corinthians 11:7-9, 11-12

Let's focus on verse seven. Without getting into a tangent discussion about head coverings and such, simply focus on the last part of verse seven where it says, "... woman is the glory of man." The word "glory" carries several meanings, such as dignity, praise, and honor. To say such about woman – that she is the glory (dignity, praise, and honor) of man – might sound ludicrous. But that's because we commonly think of "glory" as a religious word. However, First Corinthians 11:7 says what it says, in your Bible and in mine, in most translations.

We often only consider the word *glory* in terms of God's glory. Or we often think of glory as referring to Heaven. We might declare, "Our great-grandparents have gone on to *Glory*!"

Acceptable definitions of "glory" include "very great praise, honor, or distinction; resplendent beauty or magnificence; a state of great splendor; to exult with triumph; rejoice proudly; the splendor and bliss of heaven; heaven."[3] These definitions indicate that the word *glory* denotes a thing, an action, and a place.

Likewise, the word glory as it is used in the Bible is a noun, a verb, and a place or state of being. Glory in the Bible is not always associated with God, although the overwhelming use of the word refers to His splendor, majesty, power, holiness, wisdom, omnipresence, grace, and all of the other qualities that characterize Him as "God."

The use of glory as a *verb* can be seen in Romans 5:3, where it states "... but we also glory in tribulations..." We see use of the word glory as a *noun* **not** associated with God in Matthew 4:8, where it mentions "all the kingdoms of the world, and the glory of them," as well as in Luke 12:27, where the Lord Jesus says, "... Solomon in all his glory was not arrayed like one of these."

Finally, we see the use of the word glory as a *state/place of existence* in First Corinthians 15:43, where we read about the physical body being "...sown in dishonor... raised in glory..." Also in Philippians 4:19, it says, "And my God shall supply all your need according to His riches in glory by Christ Jesus."

In First Corinthians 11:7, we read that man is the glory of God. That's the esteem that God places on man, who represents the crowning epitome of God's wonderful creation. Then verse seven declares that woman is the glory of man. To use the common definitions of the word glory, we can say that woman represents the very great honor or distinction, resplendent beauty, magnificence, and great splendor of man. That's saying something very wonderful about *woman*! This conveys a powerful estimation of *woman's* value.

The remaining verses from First Corinthians that I quoted above share how man and woman are intricately connected. However, I love how verse twelve culminates the discourse with "... all things are from God."

In summary, the passage states that it is all God's design how man and woman are positioned in His scheme of creation. We can liken man to a glistening, golden crown, and woman as bedazzling jewels adorning the crown. The golden crown is simply brilliant and glorious in its own right. But the sparkling jewels mounted in it make the crown indescribably magnificent. That's an analogy of the relationship between man and woman, by God's design. In God's creation, man is special. Woman is uniquely special. Woman is the glory of man.

I reiterate that this is not to make us feel good as women. This is to help us appreciate God's objective in creating *woman*. It is imperative that we see ourselves in the light of God's perspective so that we are empowered to stand in that place and walk in that light. It is not so that we take pride in it, or "glory" in ourselves. We should attribute all glory to God, in all His glory, for the glory He has bestowed upon us through His infinite wisdom and grace.

Part II *Curse: Common Problem*
5 Punitive Situation

Genesis 3:13
And the LORD God said to the woman, "What is this you have done?" The woman said, "The serpent deceived me, and I ate."

Let's now look into the causes for some mutual challenges we face as women today. I classify the challenges under the category of our "common problem." That problem can be considered a "punitive situation." Our mutual challenges as women originated from the curse in Genesis chapter three. My opening Scripture reference, Genesis 3:13, records God's sorrowful question spurred by the man and woman's partaking of the forbidden fruit.

The woman and man did something that God forbade them to do. Because the gravity of the transgression was so great – that is, disobeying God thus coming to the knowledge of good and evil – God felt obligated to impose a perpetual reminder to all of those involved in the wrongdoing. The lasting reminder affected them, their descendants, and even the earth itself. The curse pronounced as punishment for disobedience was to be a memorial of the paradise man and woman forfeited until we again regain paradise in God's final plan for mankind.

We find the curse upon woman in verse sixteen of chapter three:

> *To the woman He said: "I will greatly multiply your sorrow and your conception; in pain you*

> *shall bring forth children; your desire shall be for your husband, and he shall rule over you."*
> *Genesis 3:16*

This is significant, because now we come to a pivotal juncture explaining why we as women have some formidable challenges, even today. I'm hoping that by the time I complete this section, and the remainder of the book, that you will have hope of how to regain your place of power and control that you were designed to possess alongside man, overcoming the effects of the curse as much as possible.

Perhaps some of you might be saying, "But Christ has redeemed us from the curse of the law, having become a curse for us" (Galatians 3:13). But may I submit to you that the curse in Genesis was declared prior to the law ever being established? May I submit to you that the curse in Genesis cannot therefore be considered the curse of the law? The curse of the law and the curse in Genesis are not the same. The law and its curses came from God through Moses. The pronouncement of curses in Genesis came directly from God with no middleman.

As further proof that we are still under the curse in Genesis chapter three, let's look at what happened after Adam and Eve disobeyed God and ate from the tree of the knowledge of good and evil:

> [14]*So the LORD God said to the serpent: "Because you have done this, you are cursed more than all cattle, and more than every beast of the field; on your belly you shall go, and you shall eat dust all the days of your life."*

16To the woman He said: "I will greatly multiply your sorrow and your conception; in pain you shall bring forth children; your desire shall be for your husband, and he shall rule over you."

17Then to Adam He said, "Because you have heeded the voice of your wife, and have eaten from the tree of which I commanded you, saying, 'You shall not eat of it': cursed is the ground for your sake; in toil you shall eat of it all the days of your life."

18"Both thorns and thistles it shall bring forth for you, and you shall eat the herb of the field."

19"In the sweat of your face you shall eat bread till you return to the ground, for out of it you were taken; for dust you are, and to dust you shall return."

Genesis 3:14, 16-19

May I ask a few questions, given the content of the curses in these Scriptures?

Does the serpent/snake still crawl on its belly today?

Does mankind still have to work, as a whole, to obtain sustenance from the land? I'm talking about mankind in general, not particular individuals. But even for people who don't work outright, *someone* has to work to produce sustenance for the rest of us. For instance, for those living on welfare, there are those who work and pay taxes. For those that inherit wealth, *someone* in their family worked, or *someone* administers their family's possessions or businesses. *Someone* has to toil in oil fields, on farms, in manufacturing facilities, on computers that run everything else, and in banks or accounting departments of mega-corporations.

Consider the excessive hours that some people work – fifty, sixty, and more hours per week – to provide for their families' needs. Some people even labor on multiple jobs to make ends meet. And some of them work under stress, in sweat shops, or under bodily duress. It takes toil to obtain our living from the earth.

Additionally, mankind has to grapple with nature to produce food in agricultural endeavors. Even with modern agricultural technology, we constantly combat weather threats and pests that destroy food crops. Inclement weather produces floods, freezes, and droughts which diminish agricultural harvests.

So the "sweat of your face" and "thorns and thistles will it bring forth for you" parts of the curse upon the earth and man are still in effect, I would say. Would you agree?

As final evidence that we are still under the curse of Genesis chapter three, may I submit that, barring medical procedures, women still have pain in childbirth? And even with medical procedures, the pain remains. It is simply not felt as acutely because of anesthetics and analgesics.

I realize that this topic about the curse is probably difficult to stomach (no pun intended). But it is nonetheless part of our unique experience as women. It is one of the three conditions affecting our journey in this life.

However, the curse concerning pain in childbearing does not constitute the entire curse upon women. Pain in childbirth is a passing affliction – and thank God for that. But the other parts of the curse affect the vast majority of us throughout our lives – even those who might not bear children. Therefore, we absolutely must devise strategies to deal with the *curse*.

We are indeed the products of creation, the curse and culture. So if we want to seize our right to wholeness, dignity, and significance, we have to comprehend our unique experience as women. That experience includes the curse in Genesis chapter three.

So with that in mind, let's move on to what I really wanted to share concerning women and the curse of Genesis chapter three. The next two chapters will explore two facets of the curse with which most of us struggle – even those who may never have experienced multiplied pain in childbirth.

Part II *Curse: Common Problem*
6 Perpetual Sensitivity

Genesis 3:16c
...your desire shall be for your husband...

Statistics today would most likely show that instances of marriage, especially for women in their twenties, are much lower when compared to their older generational counterparts at that age. The institution of marriage among Americans has been declining for several decades. There is much speculation concerning the reasons why, but they are beyond the scope of this book.

However, despite the marriage statistics, I surmise that it would be safe to say that most women envision a significant other in their lives at some point during their lives – whether they marry him or cohabitate. For Christian women seeking to follow the Biblical example, we envision ourselves as being married to our man, not simply living with him in what is commonly called "shacking up" or more simply, "shacking."

For most Christian women, a desire to marry at some point in our lives is normal and typical, even in our modern culture. I think it is safe to say that Christian women who are not emotionally damaged or hardened in some way find the attention of a man to be very important in their lives. We find validation of our womanhood to be euphoric when fostered by a man who "chooses" us. Unless there is some kind of departure from conventional womanhood, most of us have a desire for a special relationship with a gentleman in some fashion, at some point, in our lives. Some might not want a ring on the finger, but at some point, most at least contemplate it, even if we never marry. The desire is still there.

In fact, some ladies desire a relationship of this nature so strongly that they endure emotional or physical abuse while in some relationships. Although some abusive situations have extenuating circumstances that preclude the woman's desire to end the relationship, onlookers often wonder why a woman would stay in an abusive relationship. Or people wonder why a woman would stay in a relationship with a man who shows little sense of responsibility as the "man of the house."

There is just *something* about being wanted, valued, or affirmed by a man. The phrase "perpetual sensitivity" is how I choose to describe it. There is a particular, lasting vulnerability of women to men, especially in the context of romantic relationships. It's part of our common problem, particularly when it is out-of-balance in our lives.

In my opinion, this originates from our creation for relationship, as well as from Genesis 3:16, which accentuated it even more: "...your desire shall be for your husband." Now before someone takes issue with my intimating that this desire is part of the *curse*, let me clarify by expressing the following reminder: this book is about why we as women are the way we are, and why we experience the things we do, in the way we experience them. This book is about what we can do to get beyond those things which limit us from being whole and healthy, particularly in our soul (the mind, intellect, and emotions). My ambition is to provide answers for how we can receive healing in situations that exploit our shared vulnerabilities as women.

Allow me to state that the desire to be validated, affirmed, or simply valued by a man or by men in general is normal, accepted, and expected in our traditional society. To have such a desire is not a "curse" in the detrimental sense of the word. But there is the possibility for that longing to become detrimental. When the desire for a man becomes inordinately unbalanced compared to other areas of our lives, then the situation becomes a concern. When the yearning results in a forfeiture of rational thought, it's a problem. When the desire overwhelmingly diminishes our value of life, it is then that the condition needs a remedy. I want to provide insight into how we can maintain balance and a sense of well-being in our relationships, despite the counterforces surrounding us.

This book was not written to disparage or criticize women. I am a woman, and subject to all of the challenges that we all face. Neither was this book written to espouse antiquated ideas of womanhood, nor to promote postmodern feminist concepts at the other end of the spectrum.

I believe God has given me something to say that will bring healing and deliverance to my sisters in Christ. I hope that I can offer insight from a unique perspective that will help ladies find freedom and healing rather than continue to experience guilt, shame, low self-esteem, and unfulfillment. So please remain mindful of my sentiments as we move on.

At this juncture, I feel I need to look at another translation of the foundational Scripture for this chapter. Instead of stating "your desire shall be for your husband," the other translation of Genesis 3:16 states that the woman shall desire *to rule over* her husband. And although that potentially could be a proper translation, I have looked at the rendering of this verse in ten Bible translations. Only one translation rendered the condition of the woman as wanting to rule over, or to control, her husband. The other nine translations rendered this part of the curse as the woman desiring, longing for, or wanting to please, her husband.

I tend to lean toward the consensus among the nine translations, although I'm sure there are women who desire to control their husbands – and possibly everyone else, upon consideration of those types of women. But the overwhelming consensus of translations is that a woman will have a perpetual sensitivity in longing for attention, admiration, affection, and affirmation from her husband or a man in whom she might be romantically interested. This seems to hold true in societies over the centuries, and holds true today in our modern U.S. society. (Of course, I'm referring to conventional, Biblically-sanctioned romantic relationships.)

It is fascinating that the first desire we see for *woman* is a desire that inspired her to disobey God's command, however. Let's take a look at Scripture:

> *So when the woman saw that the tree was ... a tree **desirable** to make one wise, she took of its fruit and ate.*
>
> *Genesis 3:6*

Isn't it interesting that her temptation included a desire for what she was created for in the first place? She had a desire to operate in a capacity of wisdom. Let's summarize what we've already learned in order to accentuate this fact. Woman was originally created so that man would not be *alone*, to be *adequate* as his helper, and to be *advantageous* to him as an *advanced* version of himself, to assist the man in his assignment from God. We can see that here:

> ²⁷*So God created man in His own image; in the image of God He created him; male and female He created them.*
>
> ²⁸*Then God blessed them, and God said to them, "Be fruitful and multiply; fill the earth and subdue it; have dominion over the fish of the sea, over the birds of the air, and over every living thing that moves on the earth."*
> *Genesis 1:27-28*

However, the first "desire" we see in the Bible for *woman* is her desire to be wise at the expense of obedience to God, unfortunately. On top of that, she gave some of the fruit to her husband, and he also ate it. Instead of helping the man to do the right things, she helped him to do the wrong thing. That was not the helper God designed her to be.

Therefore, if we look at each facet of the curse God pronounced on the woman, it seems as though the "curse" was to *realign* her focus upon what God originally *designed* her to be and to do. Apparently, each aspect of the curse was to sharpen awareness of her original design and purpose. She was designed to help the man, first and foremost, assisting him to fill the earth, and to rule over it at his side.

The "curse" declared upon woman, then, equates to a poignant affirmation of her original purpose. The reasoning seems to be that both needed perpetual memorials of why God created them in the first place, until His ultimate consummation of what He planned for the earth and mankind.

Woman was a *helper* or a co-laborer, to be under the leadership of the man. She was created to care for God's creation *with* the man as leader. Simply put, she was to help populate the earth through childbirth, and to take charge of the earth alongside the man. So far we've seen that the subsequent curse involved pain in childbirth, and a longing for her husband (or a man) in her life.

I believe this part of the curse is how the tables turned such that it is women who genuinely dread the condition of being alone. The incessant longing or perpetual sensitivity is what compels many women to succumb repeatedly to unfulfilling relationships time-after-time. It's almost as if all sense of well-being and self-preservation is lost in the "quest for love." It is more of a compulsion or obsession in some cases. At these levels, we can see the deleterious consequence of the declaration "...your desire shall be for your husband." It is clearly displaying the characteristics of a curse in such instances. Consider the Samaritan woman who Jesus spoke to at the well, as recorded in John 4:5-18. She'd had five husbands and the man she was in a relationship with at that time was not her husband.

We will look at ways to address the effects of the curse later in the book. For now, my first job is to expose the obstacles to wholeness, dignity, and significance. My challenge is to persuade you to acknowledge the existence of these obstacles from the correct perspective, first and foremost.

I believe the preoccupation that women have with "your desire shall be for your husband" is more than obvious! The sheer amount of "how-to" advice on relationships and romance in magazines, on the Internet, in books, on radio, in podcasts, in advertisements, and on television are proof of the obsession. If the market wasn't there, the products wouldn't be there, would you agree? It's a simple case of supply and demand.

Telltale titles like "How to Please a Man," "How to Keep Your Man Happy," "How to Win a Man's Heart," and multitudes of similar titles bombard us on the magazine racks in the grocery store check-out aisles. We constantly see topics such as these in banner ads on the web sites we frequent. Titles like "The Five Things Every Man Needs" and the like are sure to get click-throughs.

There are entire industries built upon romance – entertainment thrives on it. Soap operas are still as popular as ever. Romance novels have seen no waning in their popularity, either. Statistics show that eighty-six percent of the audience for such fare consists of women.[4] I think "your desire shall be for your husband" is very easy to see in our society. The inordinate preoccupation with gaining the affirmation or love of the male of the species is indeed evidence of the curse in effect, even into this twenty-first century. I believe the incessant and exorbitant fixation toward equipping the female in the "hunt" is certain evidence of an engrossing expression of the curse in our society. Just look at how much advertising is focused on making ourselves appealing to the opposite sex. What more is there to be said about this? The evidence is overwhelming.

Of course, the rationales for establishing the marriage relationship are plenteous for women. But the foundational incentives came first from creation, and then Genesis chapter three which declares, "… your desire shall be for your husband."

In the next chapter, we'll see that the final part of woman's curse is actually a blessing if properly discerned and observed in its outworking. The dilemma, however, is that it has not been properly interpreted and administered due to the cultural shortcomings both inside and outside of the church.

Part II *Curse: Common Problem*
7 Presiding Superintendent

Genesis 3:16d
... And he shall rule over you.

Now we hit a topic that might cause the hairs of our female heads to stand up. We are about to discuss another facet of *woman's* common problem originating with the curse of Genesis 3:16. This topic surrounds the phrase, "and he shall rule over you."

And perhaps some of you were about to lay this book down, never to read another page, after chapter six. And now chapter seven's foundational Scripture has caused your blood pressure to rise and your eyebrow to twitch. Perhaps the current Scripture reference is the last straw for you, and this book is no longer worth reading as far as you're concerned.

But hold on. Remember that we are trying to determine the conditions affecting *woman's* unique journey. Therefore, we want the truth, first and foremost. And before I'm done, you'll realize that what you've been thinking or have been taught as truth might need to be adjusted a little bit. (Well, maybe a lot for some of you!) Second, don't you want to know how to benefit from the framework that surrounds our unique journey as women in this earth?

I refuse to allow others' misguided interpretations to dictate my ultimate outcome of victory! Perhaps you feel the same way. I hope you do, because I want to provide an example that will clarify the remainder of "the curse" a bit more, before I fully delve into this chapter's topic.

As a bit of comfort to you, consider this chapter's title, "Presiding Superintendent." Say it out loud: presiding superintendent. It has a ring of benevolence to it, doesn't it? Say it again. Presiding superintendent. It doesn't sound like a dictator, does it? It doesn't carry the connotation of an arrogant, insensitive, egotistical, insensitive brute, does it? *Presiding superintendent*.

Keep that in mind as we move on. Because "he shall rule over you" is analogous to saying "he shall be your presiding superintendent." That is part of the curse because there is an element of submission. However, submission can be a true blessing if instituted within God's anticipated design. It is a true curse if the parties neither accept nor understand God's design, however.

Let's investigate a comparable situation.

Consider this scenario. You are the parent of two kids: one, a twelve-year-old boy and the other, a six-year-old girl. The 6-year-old is taking a nap. So you instruct the 12-year-old to do his chores, and to go awaken the 6-year-old after you leave so she can also do her chores. You have to run to the next door neighbor's house for a quick errand. Let's imagine that you instruct the 12-year-old, "Do not turn on the television, and stay off of the Internet while I'm gone. Start doing your chores, and I'll return shortly. We can do some fun things together as a family when I return."

You leave and the 12-year-old goes to awaken his little sister to tell her to do her chores by your instruction. He instructs her to stay away from the TV and the computers. But the six-year-old decides to get on the Internet to play a game, but needs the twelve-year-old's involvement to login and to play the game. She turns on the big screen TV, and the game console, and enlists her big brother to help her. The twelve-year-old knows better than to disobey, but he decides to help her and play also. So they both disobey you.

You come home to find them playing a game. So you ground them both and tell the six-year-old, "Since you can't govern yourself, you now have to defer to your brother."

And then you tell the twelve-year-old, "You are the eldest. You should've known better. Now you have the responsibility of looking after yourself and your sister. I'm leaving you in charge from now on until I change it. So now you have to not only do your chores and homework, you're responsible for making sure your little sister does her chores and for helping her do her homework – no excuses. I will hold you responsible to a greater degree from now on, because you chose disobedience with your eyes wide open. Things will be harder for you because you now have added responsibilities – not just for yourself, but to lead, and be responsible for your sister's compliance with my directives, as well. Therefore things will be harder for you because you were influenced to disobey me when you knew to do better."

That's what happened with Adam and Eve, in a nutshell. Things became harder for them both because they disobeyed God.

But consider the story above, in which the little sister represents Eve. As a parent, you know the twelve-year-old boy knows more about you and life than what the six-year-old girl knows of either. You know the twelve-year-old understands more about obedience and disobedience, and what the potential ramifications are of disobeying you. You know the twelve-year-old understands more than the six-year-old about why they shouldn't play in the street. You know the twelve-year-old understands more about why they shouldn't talk to strangers. You know the twelve-year-old knows more about why they need to eat their vegetables and not eat a bag full of candy before dinner. The elder boy knows more about the dangers on the Internet than does his little sister.

You, as the parent, are in essence protecting the six-year-old by placing her under the caring eye of her older brother. But both she and he feel it's a burden. Both he and she hate it – *if* the boy understands the full ramifications of it; if not, he sees it as an opportunity to "be the boss." That's the wrong attitude. And that is not your intention, either. Your change is for the protection of both of them.

You know the vulnerabilities of the little girl. You are aware of the perils of her environment. You know the strengths of the son and the extent of his knowledge about their environment. You know the boy's potential to accomplish more, and you assign more responsibility to him for that reason.

That's a much simplified version of what happened with Adam and Eve. Adam had been in God's presence longer. How much longer, we do not know. But the first thing Eve saw was God then Adam. Adam had seen a lot more. He had experienced being among all the animals, and so on. The man had opportunity to converse with God about naming the animals, and personally received the commands from God about what he could and could not eat, and so on. We don't know how long these interactions occurred. We don't know when God told Adam about the tree of the knowledge of good and evil. We can only surmise that Adam had been on the earth longer, and had seen more things in his environment for a longer period of time than had Eve. Adam had interacted with God for a longer period.

So after the man and woman disobeyed, God (the protective parent, in His infinite wisdom) issued the new rules of engagement for the man and woman. In determining a way for both the man and the woman to carry out His plan that was instituted *from the beginning* and *had not changed* (that's important), He placed perpetual reminders in both of their lives – and that of their progeny, for ages to come – pointing to the error that should always keep us mindful of Him and the critical nature of obedience to Him. He placed the woman in protective custody of her husband. "And he shall rule over you" is like a curse because many married couples in Christ simply do not understand the responsibilities and ramifications of God's purpose in what He instituted.

I stress that it is more of a responsibility, rather than an advantage or entitlement, for the man to be head of his wife. The reason it has such a distaste to some women, and is gloated over by some men, is because neither understands the gravity of what God intended for it to represent. The husband is to be the presiding superintendent. It's a role of protection and covering, rather than one of control, so to speak. And the reason why it's such a burden and not executed in the way it was intended is because of the next section of this book, "culture." And we'll discuss that topic in due time.

So moving forward, associate Genesis 3:16d – that is, "... he shall rule over you" – with the words "and he shall be the presiding superintendent over you." The man was to look after his wife, protecting her, and being a guardian for her – because that's the heart of our Father for us.

In fact, Adam was not only to be the presiding superintendent over Eve after their disobedience, but going back to God's original plan, over *all* that was created *from the beginning*. That was the plan for man, and after they disobeyed, it was still the plan. That plan did not change. It just so happens that when they were caught in their sin, neither the man nor woman took responsibility. Eve blamed the serpent. Adam initially vacated his position of authority by not taking charge of the situation when approached by Eve enticing him to sin. Then he later abandoned his responsibility by blaming God.

So after their disobedience, the woman was more expressly placed under the presiding superintendent's responsibilities. As the weaker, more sensitive, more vulnerable vessel of the two, she officially obtained protective covering as explicitly stated by God in Genesis 3:16d. *From the beginning*, she was *fashioned* and *made* more sensitive, vulnerable, impressionable, and fragile because of the role that the woman was created to fulfill. She simply ended up exposing vulnerability to the wrong influence, unfortunately (the wily serpent).

And that, my sisters, ironically is what happens far too much to us today, as well. We expose our vulnerabilities to the wrong person or wrong *type* of person. We were designed to be more vulnerable, more fragile, and more sensitive. It simply was accentuated after the curse.

It does not mean *woman* is inferior. It does not mean she is less intelligent. It does not mean that she is anything less of whatever is necessary to fulfill her purpose.

She was intentionally *made* so that man wouldn't be alone. She was specifically *made* as adequate for the responsibilities they had been given. She was unequivocally *made* to be advantageous to him. She was purposefully *made* from advanced material – material into which God had already imparted His life and Spirit (that is, the man).

She was expressly *made* more fragile. I do not believe the term "weaker vessel" in describing the wife (1 Peter 3:7) is only referring to her lower level of physical strength compared to the man, or to the fact that the original woman, Eve, was deceived by the serpent when the man was not deceived. Woman was *made* weaker or more vulnerable in many respects than the man *from the beginning* because of God's purpose for her. God *designed* her to experience emotions more intensely. He *designed* her to be more relationship-oriented and vulnerable because *woman* is the nurturer and child-bearer. God *designed* her to be more delicate and sensitive because of her purpose.

We can compare "woman" to silk that you would not toss into the washing machine on heavy duty cycle with denim jeans. Silk is weaker than denim for the purpose the fabric serves. But silk is not inferior to denim.

So after their act of disobedience, the woman became even *more* vulnerable and exposed, as did the man. But their fallen state was more pressing upon her because she was *made* more delicate *from the beginning* of her existence. So, her husband was designated the presiding superintendent over her as well as the other elements of God's creation, as a protective and preservative measure following their disobedience to God's command.

The reason we bristle at "...he shall rule over you" is because, all this time, we've had the wrong idea of what it meant. And much of the disagreeable connotation for that Scripture emerged from what we'll discuss in the next segment of this book: our culture and its common particularities as it concerns women. The distaste arose as a result of cultural bias in our society-at-large as well as in the church.

So are you ready to venture into the enormous maze of culture that complicates the journey of women back wholeness, dignity, and significance?

Yes? Then let us go forth, my fearless ladies. Let us go forth.

Part III *Culture: Common Particularities*
8 Layered Social Environment

> **Psalm 1:1**
> **Blessed is the man who walks not in the counsel of the ungodly, nor stands in the path of sinners, nor sits in the seat of the scornful...**

It is time now to hogtie an unwieldy beast. I feel that I must warn you as we go forward. In the next few chapters, I will challenge ideas that our culture treats as trivial and acceptable, but which create a potentially detrimental environment for our well-being as women.

I won't be challenging Biblical boundaries – absolutely not. I'm pretty much a stickler for the overriding doctrines of God's Word. So rest assured that I will be in agreement with the word of God. This chapter's reference Scripture is evidence of my intention concerning the subject. Psalm 1:1 reminds us that there are counsels, paths, and mind-sets which are contrary to our walk with God. The opposing ideas surround us daily, and we have the opportunity to accept them or to reject them. But per the Scripture, we are blessed or empowered to be successful if we do not allow ourselves to be seduced or desensitized by the ideologies, philosophies, and opinions that are contrary to God's ways and thoughts.

There are societal and ideological dogmas that I seek to dismantle in what follows. What I say might challenge your devotion to cultural norms that we take for granted. Be mindful of this. When I challenge them, my point is not to get you to abandon them *per se*. But I want you to consider their value versus the potential damage they do to our emotional or psychological well-being as women. What I share in these chapters about culture might make you think *she's going a bit overboard here*. And I might go overboard, indeed. But there is a method to my madness.

Remember my statement from a previous chapter. I stated that if I can get you to ask the right questions, it would be a tremendous milestone in your journey toward wholeness, dignity, and significance.

I hope you're reconsidering personal mentalities about the value of "woman" in a new light even now, given what you've read so far. That is, I hope discussion of God's wondrous creation of *woman* – you – has brought unique illumination upon how you view yourself already. I hope you see how elements of the curse have shaped your desires, expectations, and vulnerabilities. And I hope that what you will read in the remaining chapters will provide even greater understanding. Remain open to thinking differently.

Please be reminded once more that although I have a predisposition to seeing women healed who might be struggling in many ways, my point is not to make anyone feel *good*. My aim is to make us feel *God*. I want to help each and every woman to see herself from God's perspective. In order to get the most out of life and out of our relationships, we need to understand our elite role from God's view. We are on a journey back to wholeness, dignity, and significance. God's perspective is paramount to a successful journey.

But we will not be able to see ourselves from God's viewpoint if we carry the baggage imposed upon us from those foreign to the female experience. Neither will we be able to view ourselves from God's vantage point if we're still dragging balls-and-chains that we, as females, place upon ourselves.

For us to walk in God's vision for His created *woman*, we must prepare ourselves to come face-to-face with norms that are common within our society. But the norms are not altogether harmless. Those societal paradigms form tapestries that can keep us in bondage to emotional, physical, and mental cycles of pain. Therefore I must touch where it hurts, so to speak, in order to remove the stinger and allow our wounds to heal.

Our culture injects some very strong ideological serum into the psyches of females from very early in our socialization. We perpetuate the cycles generationally. But we need to comprehend the gravity of our plight. We truly need to realize what we are *doing* – and what is being done *to* us – via subconscious and subliminal cultural programming from very early stages of our socialization as females in our society.

Let me give a few examples to illustrate what I'm saying. I'll subsequently return to a deeper discussion later.

A few years ago, a particular rhythm-n-blues songstress was gaining tremendous popularity. The diva became well known for her provocative dance moves and attire. A male friend of mine had seen a video that he thought was cute. He sent me a link to the video. In the video, music from the immensely popular R&B diva began to play. The video scene initially showed only a large box in what looked like someone's living room. But as the music played, a toddler – perhaps only two to three years old, wearing big afro puffs – suddenly broke out of the box and began to dance. Now, my male friend, who is a Christian, thought it was cute. I thought it was a sad commentary on what we call cute for girl toddlers.

She was being taught, as a toddler, that she was supposed to be popping out of boxes and dancing for the entertainment of others.

Years ago, my hometown hosted an annual community-sponsored Martin Luther King, Jr. Day parade. The city ultimately discontinued the parade as we knew it, and replaced it with a city-sponsored event. However, during the parade's early years, specific types of dance troupes would make an annual appearance. The dance troupes usually were curated by men. The dancers were all girls, however, ranging in age from elementary school to junior high school. The girls had been taught to dance like video vixens, with highly provocative gyrations of their hips and torsos. Again, culture was teaching these girls that dancing provocatively was expected of them, and worthy of cheers in public places.

There is currently a colloquial phrase going around that pokes fun at someone by declaring, "You _____ like a girl." (Fill in the blank – run, throw, catch, scream, etc.) In other words, if you do something "like a girl," you're weak, comical, and not to be taken seriously.

These are just a few examples of the demeaning psychological programming that we experience as females. It starts when we're very young and continues to color our world into adulthood. It's so commonplace and natural that we generally allow it to continue without challenge.

As a final example, I have a disagreeable recollection of the news media's coverage of the second inaugural ball for President Barack Obama. I recall how the media's fashion aficionados cooed, chattered, and fawned over the attire of Mrs. Obama during the inaugural events. There was extremely too much attention given to how glamorous her evening gown was; who designed it; why he was chosen to design the gown; how Mrs. Obama looked in the gown; why she chose that gown, or the designer, and so on.

My eventual thoughts?

> Mrs. Obama has done much humanitarian work in her career. She earned a law degree from Harvard. She has made history as the first African-American First Lady and has entered her second term in that role. She is well-spoken. Her fortitude has not wavered while standing beside her husband who has endured disrespect that no other U.S. President has had to endure while serving in office. She holds conversations with dignitaries and educators in all echelons of our society. Her personality and charm resonate with kids of all ages, among other noteworthy attributes that characterize her life. And all they can think of to marvel about in a mini-documentary for Mrs. Obama is her **evening gown**?

My final thought on the matter was if anyone besides me saw a problem with those news people's preoccupation with drivel. Surely they could've found something of greater substance to discuss concerning Mrs. Obama during that iconic occasion. No, they chose to babble on and on about her attire.

What are incidents like these teaching our little girls? That their bodies are for the entertainment of the masses? That what we look like and what we wear are more important than who we are or anything that we've accomplished? That the elegance of a woman eclipses everything else about her? Yes, these are the types of conclusions one can deduce from such frivolous frenzies.

And what is happening as our little girls mature into teens and then into women with those mentalities? What warped mind-sets do some of them carry into adulthood? What scars are inflicted upon their emotions and psyches as little girls, and then are reinforced by "normal" societal sentiments?

I am pained deeply when I survey the incessant but sometimes subtle brainwashing that little girls undergo from the time they are toddlers. The barrage continues into our adulthood. The assault ebbs at times. But sometimes it is more blatant and forceful than at other times. This indoctrination is ingrained in our society, and there is layer-upon-layer of it. That's why I titled this chapter "Layered Social Environment." The brainwashing is layered into the fabric of our cultural socialization. Unfortunately, the indoctrination and effects thereof probably will not change for the vast majority of the female population.

However, for those who believe in Jesus Christ as Savior and Deliverer, the remedy can be injected into our hearts and minds. We can teach our little girls and young ladies the truth, and expect healing and wholeness to develop. We must dispense truth in order to counter the assault on the psyches of females.

The difficulty is that Christians – male and female – do not address the matter to any great extent. We basically approach the world's "counsels" in similar fashion to the world's mentality about the indoctrination. We dismiss the brainwashing as something that is trivial or "normal," contrary to the admonition in Psalm 1:1 to reject it.

Therefore our girl toddlers grow up to be broken little girls, who become disillusioned teens, who grow into injured young ladies, who persist into various stages of adulthood with scars that could last a lifetime. The result is illustrated by unhealthy coping mechanisms, such as anorexia, depression, codependency, combativeness, and low self-esteem to name a few. We can end up in broken relationships repeatedly throughout our lives, experiencing compounded injury and deeper damage to emotions.

I'm not a psychologist. And I'm not trying to be one, although much of what I say has psychological roots and ramifications. I am simply an observer of the society in which we live.

But I'm a little more by God's call. I'm one who cries aloud and spares not, by a mandate of the Lord. I see the things done in the dark and shout them from the rooftops. And finally, I am just a woman emerging from those same aforementioned cultural trappings to gain God's perspective.

It is a serious matter to counter the world's ideologies that are injected into the minds of girls at an early age. We must begin to address the issues while girls are young. By the time the propaganda comes to full fruition, there are numerous effects that incapacitate some women to the point of dysfunction in some instances. Or, the brainwashing proliferates causing abated hopes of happiness at best, as we mature.

Allow me to state again that the detrimental ideologies emanate from our *culture*. The ideologies are widespread and unavoidable in normal day-to-day living because they are ingrained in our culture. They are ubiquitous within society and woven into numerous aspects of daily living. Therefore we must be cognizant of the influences, however subtle the subconscious ideas might be. Ultimately, we must enact counteractive measures to keep the young psyches and emotional states of our girls protected and healthy.

Culture – our societal environment – is one of the most powerful contributors to how we think, what we become, and how we respond to our surroundings. We were created for a noble purpose by God. But from an early age as females, we are indoctrinated into molds that will not reflect God's lofty intent. Our culture spawns inside of us an image of "woman" that is flawed. We consequently seek to operate in that skewed, distorted framework. But the mental architecture is faulty and unhealthy from the start.

The icon of *woman* in our culture – the one that we strive to emulate – will not blossom into God's design and original purpose for *woman*. The identity implanted in our minds as little girls routinely causes us to target petty objectives as we mature. Cultural preconceptions, into which we all are "born" as females, make us strive toward unrealistic and superficial goals, particularly as it pertains to physical appearance.

But culture also affects our ambitions and expectations of what we can achieve as adult women – or should even *attempt* to achieve. Our culture even affects what we expect from our relationships.

And therein lies the thorny challenges that sprout from the cultural soil into which we are planted as soon as we are born. The brainwashing starts when we are toddlers. But we, as believers, need to be proactive in the way that we respond. We should not let the ideologies go unchallenged. We need to inject God's perspective into the minds of girls and women. Remember God's admonition in Psalm 1:1 – we are blessed if we keep God's counsel preeminent in our lives. But if we succumb to our culture's way of thinking, we will be doomed to lives of brokenness, indignity, and feelings of insignificance.

Most assuredly, there are millions of women who live rewarding and fulfilling lives. This book was not written for them. With this book, I am seeking to bring healing to the damage that occurs to the other millions who are incapacitated by the obstacles they face – obstacles that are cultivated by our culture.

If we are honest, we will admit that we know of at least one woman who is the result of society's warped mentality. We all know of at least one woman who has been through devastating situations in relationships, or who has endured emotional injury, self-esteem issues, or who is even now operating with impaired coping strategies. Or perhaps we know someone who has come to an untimely end because of our culture's degenerate ideologies that pushed her over the edge. If it's not you who has suffered adverse consequences, it is a sister, cousin, friend, mother, aunt, grandmother, daughter, neighbor, or coworker.

We are very aware of the epidemic of dysfunction that claims female victims psychologically, physically, and emotionally on a daily basis. As a gender, we suffer the ravages of anorexia, emotional abuse, teen pregnancy, sexual abuse, bulimia, physical abuse, low self-esteem, date rape, multiple divorces, promiscuity, and so on.

We all are aware that these tragedies are the result of a world without Christ. There's no question about that. However, what about inside the Body of Christ? Do we see these issues in girls and women who are believers? Yes, we see most, if not all of the ills, in the lives of professing believers, as well. So we, as Christians, are not immune to these problems. We have failed to convey

God's perspective of who we are, how we are, and why we exist even among ourselves.

What I'd like to see among Christians is a concerted effort to counter the brainwashing put forth by our culture. What I'd like to see is a movement in the faith community *en masse* that counters the propagation of warped expectations concerning women.

We traditionally have expressed a response in terms of a sin-consciousness, such as admonishing young ladies not to dress provocatively. But addressing the causes of why these ills are prevalent in young ladies, or seeking to combat the issues head-on, is lacking in ministry to girls, young ladies, and women, by-and-large.

A few cosmetic beauty companies have taken the lead in seeking to rectify the distorted images of women proliferated in media and the arts. (Cosmetic companies, of all entities!) And a few other organizations have also joined the ranks, by producing esteem-building videos and disseminating them via social media web sites.

But our Women's Ministries are content to host fashion shows. We advertise women's ministry events that promote facials and exercise socials. Please don't get me wrong – these are nice activities and thank God for "nice" activities. But deeply embedded, injurious cultural ideas remain that the church needs to wrestle and bring under captivity to the knowledge and obedience of Christ.

God has the answer. His design for "woman" is the answer. His purpose for each one of us, singularly, and collectively, is the answer. But our injurious social adaptations muddy His plan. Our own methods of overcoming injury or coping with emotional pain subvert His comprehensive solution. And unless we cut through the smoke and mirrors instituted and supported by a warped culture, we will have little success in setting aright the minds, emotions, and hearts of women because the cultural siege starts when we're little girls.

Earlier in this chapter, I admitted that I wasn't a psychologist. But I may have sounded like one in this chapter. I wasn't attempting to do so, because I am not in the profession nor do I possess credentials in the field of psychology. However I, like most of you, have seen and experienced the psychological onslaught and its resultant emotional pillage we (as females) experience at the hands of our fallen culture.

It's time to add another voice to the rising outcry against the raging beast. This one is inspired by the One Who created us. If I can inspire some of you to run to the battle with me, slingshot in hand, we will make progress in slaying the giants that have intimidated us for so long. For our own sake, we must cut through the layered social environment. It resembles thick, dangerous underbrush in a jungle. It causes us to stumble. We've got to dismantle the layers of the environment – dissect them – to rid ourselves of that which is detrimental to our emotional health.

Part III *Culture: Common Particularities*
9 Low Self-Esteem

Psalm 3:3
But You, O LORD, *are* a shield for me, my glory and the One who lifts up my head.

As Christians, sometimes we resort to clichéd responses to societal ills. We occasionally state answers to problems in the simplest manner possible. For instance, if we were to assess an ill in our society, we might say, "It all stems from the sin problem," or "It's the result of the sin nature." We may never get to a specific remedy except to say, "Just turn it over to Jesus." Although all of those statements and advice are true and valuable, they lack specific substance upon which people can act.

We know Jesus is the answer. But I want to pose the question, "How do we make progress toward receiving His healing?" Yes, we all know that Jesus is the answer, He holds the answer, He has the answer, and He is the only answer. My question is, "How do we get His healing to become evident in our lives?" Or another way to ask the same question is, "How do we get past our issue?" Or another way to ask it might be, "How do we experience manifestation of the answer in our situation?"

We have to get past simplistic answers, as true as they are, and provide something tangible that people can grasp and do. We must offer something to hurting people that is experiential so that they truly can be healed inside.

That is critical because many women in Christ live with emotional and psychological infirmities, not the least of which is low self-esteem. I was saved, sanctified, filled with the Spirit, fire-baptized, on my way to heaven without a doubt, active in the local church, licensed, and ordained in ministry – yet still struggling with low self-esteem for many years as a Christian. And I assure you, I was not an isolated case.

Research shows that self-esteem is roughly equal in pre-adolescent boys and girls. However, as they grow older, self-esteem begins to decline steadily in both sexes, but most prevalently among teen girls. A more grim fact is that the degree of divergence between self-esteem levels for boys versus girls *accelerates* during the teen years.[5] To envision this, imagine a line graph depicting self-esteem slowly declining equally for both girls and boys at equal inclines until puberty. The older the girls get, imagine their line graph plunging downward steeply, while the boys' line graph remains in a slow steady decline through their teenage years. Stated simply, as teens age, the greater the disparity between self-esteem levels for girls compared to boys.

In my opinion, the overarching reason for the swift decline in girls' self-esteem as they enter puberty is because of the *objectification* of females. By objectification, I mean the cultural emphasis upon physical female characteristics as separate, dehumanized objects for sexualization. That is, our busts, backsides, lips, eyes, hair, legs, and so on, are valued for their "sex appeal" in our society. Our features are objects of lust and gratification outside of the totality of our personhood. There is an ideal image of *woman* that society pushes into the mainstream. Girls or women who do not match the imaginary ideal (and few do, naturally, by the way) begin to suffer from low self-esteem because of an unobtainable and unrealistic ideal they are seeking to emulate or to reflect.

But hold on. The most sobering fact is that objectification doesn't start with teenagers or women as the initial target. It starts with girl toddlers. It starts with preschool girls. It is perpetuated among kindergartners up through high school ages. It continues as we enter into middle-age. But it *started* when we were toddlers. And unfortunately, women are some of the ones who facilitate the perpetuation of objectification. It permeates every layer of our society. I listed examples in chapter eight of how toddlers and young girls are trained (as a "natural" part of growing up) how to dance in order to titillate. Objectification is a common particularity of our culture. It cultivates and contributes to the perpetuation of low self-esteem in females.

A "mild" example of the objectification that starts with little girls is beauty pageants for toddlers. *For crying out loud*, some might protest. *What's wrong with beauty pageants?*

My answer would be, first and foremost, the name. Nothing is wrong with the concept of beauty, until it is defined by the superficiality that normally is associated with the term – definitions which are arbitrary, totally subjective, and usually devoid of intrinsic value. My second contention to the pageants is a question: What is their purpose? The contestants are *toddlers*. We all probably have seen the little ones all dressed up in garb suitable for a cabaret dancer in Las Vegas, complete with makeup, figure-enhancing pads, and the like. They are *toddlers*. Objectification at an early age is all it is. It's the sexualization of toddlers, which by no means is trivial.

Our culture dictates that the female has the dubious opportunity of being objectified, beginning in preschool years, for no valid reason other than the fact it is "normal" in our society. As a society, we begin to lay the foundation for low self-esteem in girls as toddlers. That's normal, expected, and permissible according to our cultural norms.

Surely we must realize by this time that low self-esteem is the catalyst for much deviant, antisocial, and self-destructive behavior in our society, particularly among females. Eating disorders ensue because the girls see themselves as being "fat." Bullying ensues because someone takes out her own insecurities on another who is weaker. Suicide ensues because someone is bullied beyond her ability to bear. Suicide is the most permanent escape for those who live with internal pain, not the least of which is low self-esteem.

Other self-destructive fallout from low self-esteem includes immodesty, promiscuity, and "sexting" perpetrated in order to fit in or to exhibit one's "assets." Such behaviors and activities are frowned upon by the church, of course. I mean, several of the behaviors are considered sins, right?

But these young ladies have been trained since they were three years old that their value is in objectification or sexualization of their bodies. Recall my examples of the "diva toddler" and the dance troupes in chapter eight? Our culture cultivates and perpetuates mind-sets and behaviors that we repeat throughout our lives. If few seek to adjust those mind-sets in a way that shows that females have value for any other reasons, we will have neither incentive nor motivation to change.

Now I'm not saying that every toddler who was entered into a beauty pageant or who has won a pageant is going to end up on the wrong side of the tracks, so to speak. We're looking at the big picture, not individuals.

But what I *am* saying is that we take too many cultural norms for granted without assessing the potential damage they cause in children and then ultimately, teen girls and women. Beauty pageants are just one example, and a minor one at that. And even so, there is a raging debate in the secular arena as to the suitability of pageants for toddlers. Again, it's the objectification and sexualization issue that underlies the debate. But it's the secular world leading the discussion. The church is not stepping forward on the subject, for the most part.

Yet according to our opening Scripture, Psalm 3:3, God is the One Who lifts our head from the doldrums of discouragement and dejection, emotional aftereffects of low self-esteem. Christians are not immune to these emotions.

Most of us have had our own bouts with low self-esteem that emanated from the culture-at-large and its distorted idea of what it was to be a woman. Of course, the determinant attributes for "womanhood" in our culture accentuate attractiveness and sex appeal to the opposite sex. Those qualities are at the very top of the list.

The specific causes for low self-esteem are very pervasive in our culture. They are firmly embedded within the fabric of our society. And I believe most of them are the result of objectification. I believe that objectification is the intrinsic foundation for most self-esteem issues among females.

Let's open this up with some examples. I'm going to list some common objects or activities, in my opinion, that have resulted from objectification. Not all of the things I list are overtly associated with objectified thought about women. And I'm not saying that these things are "evil" or that you should burn them in a bonfire. (Please try not to read that into what I'm saying on this topic.) Try to stay unbiased. I simply want to ask you, "What is the first thought that comes to your mind when you see the following words?" The first thought only! Okay – read.

Thongs
Stiletto heels
Beauty pageants
Fashion shows
Photoshopped photos
Girlie magazines
Mini skirts
Facelifts
Fake lashes
Big hair
Botox
Breast implants
Night cream
Make-up

Now I only listed these things for one reason. They can serve to perpetuate objectification of women in our society. Do you see how many of them have to do with the physical appearance of women or accentuating some attribute of the female anatomy? (And I concede that there might be extenuating circumstances for some cosmetic procedures. I'm primarily considering those which are elective to "enhance" someone's definition of beauty.)

Now I want to ask you another question. Can you make a list of items for men that has the same effect on your thoughts? Ready? Go!

How many did you come up with, and how long did it take you? Chances are, it was a short list. Men are not objectified in our culture to any substantial extent.

When I was a little girl, I enjoyed watching the Miss America pageant more than the other beauty pageants because it required a talent portion at that time. The other pageants did not have a talent segment. The other beauty contests simply televised the young ladies walking around in heels, evening gowns, and bathing suits. (I think Miss Teen USA used to have a talent segment, but that one was not nearly as popular.) Even as a young person, I felt that women should be valued based upon more than our figure, hair, pretty faces, and fashions.

Now I'm not railing on the pageant contestants or pageants *per se*, as the winners engage in humanitarian endeavors, attend college, and display character qualities that are great for all of us to emulate. However, I am simply stating that objectification has been a major part of such contests – at least it was for the segment of the competition that was televised when I viewed them.

Now I am not (I repeat, am *not*) trying to demonize (if you will) all of the items in the previous list. I can hear some ladies now: "What's wrong with my shoes?" I chuckle as I type this, but I would be negligent of sisterly decency if I didn't share that very high stilettos were designed primarily to accentuate three parts of the female anatomy: the leg, the bust, and the rear end. They were designed to make the legs seem longer and shapelier, to jut out the bust, and to thrust the rear end upwards as the anatomy adjusts the center of balance to walking on the toes rather than the heel.

Objectification. Plain and simple. And we know that when we see the shoe styles, we think, "Ooh, that's sexy!" Or that's what wearers may want admirers to think about the shoe, or the wearer *in* the shoe. I'm laughing right now, but...

Objectification.

But I'm not trying to get you to throw out your shoes! I am trying to get us all to think about the things we take for granted in our culture, as being "just the way it is." My aim is to get us, as Christian women, to reassess the mind-sets that characterize our culture and that are ingrained in all of us as children. They pepper our way of thinking even as believers in Christ.

Let's consider how objectification contributes to our derailed journey as women. Objectification is one of the major contributors to low self-esteem in women. That is no mystery. But objectification is so pervasive in our culture that it's difficult to separate ourselves from it.

However, when we accept objectification as being "just the way it is" – or when we participate in it – we detach ourselves from analyzing it and countering its effects upon our emotions and psyches. When we lose the ability to analyze it, we lose the neutrality that is necessary to help us consider the context of what we're participating in. Such a loss of neutrality is perilous.

Individually, we need to bring neutrality to bear and think, *Wait a minute. I don't have to accept this. I don't have to continue to be objectified. God made me a certain way for a specific time. He placed me in a certain context for my purpose and destiny.*

If we don't know what God designed us for, or why, or how we're supposed to fulfill His plan, we will be swept away by the cultural tide. We potentially could be carried away into the emotional injury and psychological indignity that our culture fosters in women. We see the results reflected in the statistics surrounding the things which befall women, like pervasive low self-esteem and depression, which are more prevalent among women than among men.

Therefore let us embrace the mind-set that incites us to evaluate the trappings of objectification in our culture. I believe we can instill a healthier mind-set in our girls. It's one of the keys to protect us from culture's ideologies about women. It points us toward God's perspective concerning "woman."

Our vulnerabilities in these areas are exploited within our society by the cultural bent to objectify women. But God meant for our vulnerabilities to be covered by the "presiding superintendent" that we learned about in chapter seven. The "desire… for your husband" (soft spot to be accepted, affirmed, and appreciated by the man) was supposed to be protected by the man rather than exploited.

If you haven't yet made the connection, I repeat once more: objectification is probably the leading cause for self-esteem issues among women in our culture. And low self-esteem is the catalyst leading to numerous ills such as anorexia, overeating, codependence, lack of ambition, self-deprecation over physical appearance, depression, and a myriad of other afflictions that plague women disproportionately. Of course these issues are complex, and many factors contribute to their incidence and perpetuation.

I reiterate – I'm not telling you to throw away your stilettos and false eyelashes! However, a major concern

I have is what I've observed among Christians – men and women, alike. It seems like select entities in the secular society are doing more to repair the damaged self-esteem of girls and women than the body of Christ is doing.

All too often, we see Christians engaging in the same objectification of women as does the world – just in a less offensive way. As the owner of an Internet radio station, I've heard the lyrics of some gospel rappers whose music I've featured on the station. On a few occasions, I've heard them testify that they don't need to have mistresses for sex, instead rapping, "I have a wife for that." Now it is admirable (and expected by God) that these brothers maintain fidelity in their marriages. But is that really a reason to confess in song of why they are married?

Objectification.

For the church-at-large to have program after program, sermon after sermon, extolling the virtuous woman, but little to no training for the men of God's house on how to honor the wife as the weaker vessel, or on how to love her as Christ loves the church (a self-sacrificial love, for those who might not know what it entails), is almost akin to objectification.

Faith comes by hearing, and hearing by the Word of God. So all the Word is good and we all need to be better virtuous women. But someone should be able to receive a Word from the Lord to teach the brothers on God's way for them to grow more in the role of the protective presiding superintendent.

I have an account on the popular website Facebook.com. As a woman of God, I am continually posting Scriptures, comments, and images which point readers to spiritual matters. Rarely, if ever, do I get a comment to those kinds of posts from family or friends. But when I post photos of myself, I get comments and "likes" from numerous friends and family members without fail. In other words, it's almost as if I don't exist until I start posting photos. The vast majority of my photos' commenters are Christian friends and family, both men *and* women. But the Word of God or spiritual posts get little to no interaction. (I realize that there is some manipulation of who sees what posts on that site. But it partly is based upon what kinds of posts the viewer has liked or commented on in their history of interaction on the site.)

So by all estimations, then, Christians are flowing right along with the standards of our culture. Post a pretty face, or a shapely figure, and get comments by the bucket load. Post political commentary, scientific observations, or spiritual illumination, and the overwhelming result is to hear crickets chirping.

By our actions, we are saying that a pretty woman is to be acknowledged, first and foremost, because she's attractive. She dresses nice. Her appearance is appealing. Anything else she does or represents is of lesser value.

Yet whenever our totality as a person is disregarded, we are being objectified. Whenever our uniqueness as a person is ignored, or whenever our entirety of existence is downplayed, we are being objectified. And Christians need to take a leading, active role in promoting women's *wholeness*, dignity, and significance in the earth.

Although there is a lot we can do in the natural to raise the self-esteem of women, we cannot ignore the supernatural in seeking healing for low self-esteem. This is critically important. Recall that I shared in the beginning of this book that my healing began when I acted by faith in obedience to a minister's instruction. She instructed us to write down on a slip of paper our biggest hurt, and then to throw the note into the trash can at the front of the church, on the altar. That's what I did, and I could tell immediately that something shifted in my psyche and emotions.

Yet there are avenues we can traverse *ourselves* toward freedom and healing, as well. The knowledge that I've shared in this chapter can serve as your connection of faith. But it is only a springboard. I urge you to take action to cement the commitment. Real faith is accompanied by action.

> *For as the body without the spirit is dead, so faith without works is dead also.*
> James 2:26

Consider the concepts I have presented. Contemplate what you previously may have taken for granted as being a harmless cultural norm. Think about what you can teach your daughters, granddaughters, or sisters in Christ concerning objectification to counter its effects upon their psyches and emotions. Begin to think just a little differently.

We place so many chains on ourselves. Physical appearance is the biggest one. This is primarily driven by our culture's obsession with appearance. However, fixing up the outside has very limited effect on the inside, if the inside remains broken and is never healed. Let's be more concerned about the inside – and not simply for ourselves, but for the emotional health of our sisters, as well.

Part III *Culture: Common Particularities*
10 Labyrinthine Spiraling Emotions

Jeremiah 10:19
Woe is me for my hurt! My wound is severe. But I say, "Truly this is an infirmity, and I must bear it."

At the time of writing this book, national news is buzzing with accounts of violence against women. Current events have centered around men in the entertainment industry – sports and television celebrities – who have been accused of domestic and sexual abuse against women they have dated, or with whom they have had casual acquaintances. By the time this book is published, the news most likely will still be rift with allegations, and new stories may surface.

There has been consternation among news journalists and commentators against one of the alleged abusive men in particular because he has been reluctant to provide a public, detailed rebuttal of the allegations. He has been accused of drugging his victims, then sexually assaulting them while they were incapacitated, unable to resist his sexual advances. Numerous women have come forward singularly since the story broke, accusing the same man of similar instances of abuse with each of them. He has denied the allegations so far only through his lawyer by a simple statement.

I have a male friend who cannot comprehend why any woman who suffers sexual violation would wait several years before revealing a crime like what is being reported currently in the news. My friend suspects that some, if not all, of the women are lying about the allegations. He asked me if it made sense to reveal the assaults years later, potentially ruining a man's reputation, since the man and all of the women seem to have gone forward with their lives up until this point in time. My friend asked why a woman would get any catharsis from divulging this type of crime after such a long span of time has transpired – after everyone has apparently gone on to live normal lives. He could not believe the women could possibly be telling the truth about having been sexually violated so long ago, having carried the memory for so long in secrecy.

First and foremost, in retrospect, if the allegations are indeed true, we, as total outsiders, don't know what the assumed "normal" lives of the women have entailed to this date. For all we know, they might have been having frequent nightmares or flashbacks (if the allegations are true). Or they might have endured damaged emotions, and consequently, broken relationships as a result of their alleged assaults. We have no clue how normal or abnormal their lives have been, particularly concerning relationships. That's completely in the realm of their private lives.

But without passing judgment on whether or not the accused man or his multiple accusers are lying, I shared with my male friend that yes, a woman can hold onto such a terrible truth in her life for years before revealing it. Yes, she can live her life concealing a crime of sexual violence committed against her. Women keep silent, and have kept silent, for centuries under similar circumstances in various generations. Ultimately, I shared with my friend that if he were a woman, he would understand why such a crime could be held in secret for so long.

In fact, I shared with him that I recently had become aware of a friend who had experienced sexual assault in *her* youth. She confessed that she had told no one, and that I was the only one to whom she had revealed it. Yet the trauma it had caused was still affecting her life and relationships as an adult woman. She had not revealed her traumatic experience to anyone, and had kept it secret for decades. Yes, women do that, unfortunately.

The reasons girls and women would keep secret such horrific crimes of sexual molestation or violation are complex and numerous. The ironic thing about it is that I have never been sexually abused (thank God), but I can understand why a woman would keep it a secret. I can *identify*, even though it has never happened to me. There could be extreme shame, guilt, a debilitating sense of violation, denial, a paralyzing sense of helplessness and victimization, fear of reprisal, fear of disbelief from others, fear of judgment by others, and any number of other agonizing emotions in the aftermath of such a crime.

The emotions can spiral into a wicked maze of troublesome feelings and behaviors for *years*. This is one of the common particularities among women. Our emotions can spiral into a maze of incapacitating scenarios for us.

Perhaps my male friend could not understand why a woman would keep such crimes a secret because, in my friend's world, he has seen sex used as a tool to produce whatever ultimate benefit was desired – by both genders. Sex was a means to an end, so to speak – be it simple sexual pleasure or something else. In some social circles, both men and women engage in sex to obtain individual benefits specific to their desires. We see it in the world of celebrities and sports figures who are accustomed to having groupies around. The groupies obtain status and perks in exchange for giving the celebrities sexual gratification.

In that sense, then, we must presume that it is consensual sex on the part of both the men and women. Although their motives are possibly different, each party sees a benefit to the activity, perhaps exclusive of sensual pleasure alone.

However, when sex is not consensual, there is something very heinous and sinister about forced sexual activity. But even when it is consensual, if one person's perceived benefit does not materialize, then there could be emotional or psychological fallout. And traditionally, it has been the woman who has experienced most of the unpleasant fallout in such instances.

Please recognize I am not discussing adjudication of premarital or extramarital sex, or promiscuity, or their standing in God's sight at this point. Over the past few decades, the perception of where sex fits into relationships has gone very far away from God's plan – for both women and men. Today teen girls are engaging in premarital sex to purposefully get pregnant so that they can collect money from government programs in some instances. That's just a cold, hard fact. But I am not attempting to approach activities or mind-sets like that in this discussion. Such topics are outside of the scope of this book.

At this point, I feel I should reiterate my purpose in writing this book. I want to guard our thoughts from straying from the concepts I've presented already. We are determining how *creation,* the *curse,* and *culture* have played out in who we are, how we are, and why we exist. I don't want you to take out a magnifying glass and begin to look at things from a microscopic level when I'm trying to provide a thirty-thousand-foot panorama.

I compare my approach to having a picture puzzle before us, with puzzle pieces strewn over a coffee table, the carpet, and underneath chairs in a living room. Our culture has taken the pieces of a huge picture puzzle of "woman," separated the pieces, and flung the pieces of the puzzle this way and that way. The puzzle pieces have been left unattended and jumbled in our lives. I'm attempting to help you locate the pieces, properly position them, and assemble them so that we can comprehend the big picture from God's perspective.

An in-depth analysis of the ink quality in the picture, the shape of the puzzle pieces, or how large or small the pieces are cut is irrelevant. We just need to find the pieces and put them together to see the whole picture. Therefore we must avoid being drawn off into peripheral discussions about the puzzle pieces for which we cannot formulate answers within the context of my intent. Such discussions are extremely complex and beyond the scope of this book.

What I wanted to ultimately share in this chapter, however, is that we have to understand that although our emotions are natural and designed by God, we must realize first and foremost that as women, we have an inclination to allow our emotions to run unchecked. Sometimes they will be allowed to track so far off course that we lose a sense of reality. That's why I titled this chapter "Labyrinthine Spiraling Emotions." The word *labyrinthine* means

> *of, relating to, or resembling a labyrinth; complicated; tortuous.*[6]

For additional clarity, a *labyrinth* is defined as

> *an intricate combination of paths or passages in which it is difficult to find one's way or to reach the exit.* 7

Would you agree that our emotions can sometimes be comparable to a labyrinth – a complicated maze – from which it is difficult to emerge sometimes? And would you agree that our emotions can spiral out of control and cause further injury to ourselves and others? Our own emotions torture us above and beyond the boundaries of what actually happens to us, when we rehearse, relive, and rehash the occurrences. It's difficult to find our way out of the pain sometimes, long after incidents have passed.

Passionate outward expression is part of the fabric of our society, especially for women. But we also find that implosion under the full weight of our emotions can be as common. Implosion is an inward collapse with forcefulness, as contrasted with an explosion. So instead of an emotional outburst, emotional implosion describes emotions that cave in internally, trapping us into being silent. Implosion is a contributor to how a woman can be silent for decades about a sexual assault committed against her.

Of course, sexual assault is not the only experience that can send our emotions into a tailspin. Varying degrees of infirmity can result from emotional roller coasters in our lives, such as bad relationships. The level of infirmity can range from minor irritation to complete breakdown or depression.

A critical realization is that the time to take action is when we first recognize that our emotions are about to take us for a wild ride. Responses to allay any emotional time bomb include prayer and getting clarification about the upsetting stimulus. Misunderstandings have caused many unwarranted emotional reactions. We can always speak the Word of life over our situation. And finally, we can solicit professional counseling. And I repeat – the best time to take action is before our emotions have a chance to incapacitate us.

I feel the need to clarify that I am not speaking of emotional challenges resulting from neurotic disorders. Those may require professional assistance to alleviate them.

I am referring to the general tendency we have as women to let our emotions run rampant, just from things that happen in our everyday lives. This book addresses challenges that most of us battle universally as women – battles that keep us in cycles of defeat, despair, or discouragement, especially as it pertains to relationships.

There is nothing wrong with the healthy expression of emotions. And by healthy, I mean weeping, laughing, or even expressing anger or displeasure in healthy ways. The brains of women are physiologically and chemically wired to experience emotions more intensely than men. We need to recognize that God gave us this design. As women, we are the nurturers, we are the encouragers, and we are the "tender hearts." Thus God gave us a wider palette of emotional faculties *by design*, so that we have the capability to empathize with others in our roles as mothers, encouragers, and nurturers of young ones and the vulnerable.

This is not to say that men do not operate with the capacity for wide emotional expression. They can, and thank God, many do or can shift into these roles when necessary. But as women, we are naturally more inclined to operate in these modes *by design*. This is the reason why women can remember more details about emotionally-charged events. Scientists have discovered that events that trigger emotional responses are etched into our memories more effectively. Since we (as women) routinely run on emotional "high octane" chemicals in our brains all the time, it's easier for us to remember details about events that incite emotional responses.

So it's okay to cry. It's okay to want to talk through problems or just "talk." It's okay to express a longing for security. It's okay to want to be protected. Our hormones and brains have been created with a propensity toward these things. And the "presiding superintendent" should have plenty of opportunity to perform his role in these instances, if he's properly doing what he was charged by God to do.

But our emotional expressions become unhealthy when we veer off into the perilous territory of labyrinthine spiraling emotions. Our emotions become a maze of trouble when they are uncontrolled. They form a labyrinth of destructive proportions when they take us down a path of depression, rational imbalance, unwarranted fears, extreme insecurity, codependency, and low self-esteem. Or conversely, they are just as dangerous when they convert us into a hardened, abrasive controller. A caustic demeanor is just as damaged as a weak, codependent disposition. Both conditions of dysfunction are indicative of a person who has sought her own unhealthy means of coping with injury, neglect, or lack of proper care during times of vulnerability in her life.

I've been managed by a few female bosses in my past. It is rumored that women make the worst bosses. That is a prejudiced and untrue statement, although I admit that one female boss was the opposite of what I would've wanted in a boss of any gender. I've also had a couple of male bosses like that. But another female boss was among the best bosses who ever managed me. Coincidentally, two of my female bosses had nervous breakdowns. It's reported that one of them even attempted to commit suicide.

One of those poor ladies had grown up in a physically-abusive home. Her biological dad was an abusive husband and father. My manager carried her fears of abusive men into adulthood. During the time I worked for her, her manager's boss embodied her abusive father's persona, in her opinion. She endured self-inflicted fear and stress over performing adequately for her manager's boss to such an extent that after she quit that job, she could not bring herself to search for another job. Ultimately, she developed a stress-induced eating disorder and could not digest solid food. She only drank liquids – infrequently, at that. She basically starved herself, and eventually had a stroke which took away some of her ambulatory ability.

When I visited her a few years after her stroke, it was agonizing to watch her. We were the same age, but she moved like an elderly lady – gingerly and in an unsteady manner with a cane. This occurred because she allowed her emotions to spiral out of control in response to everyday stresses that we all face. Her emotional challenge ultimately progressed into a neurotic disorder, culminating in a medical condition and ultimate physical disability. That is utterly tragic.

She could have quelled the issue when it was still an emotional response had she realized she was a marvel that God designed. Her unhealthy view of herself came from her earthly father. But her Heavenly Father was there all along, desiring to show her the value of what He created her to be.

Oh – did I forget to mention that she was a Christian? The manager was a Christian and one of the best managers I ever had. But she had no clue how to deal with feelings of insecurity, fear, intimidation, and disapproval. Those feelings more than likely originated in her childhood as she was being raised by an abusive dad. And they were projected onto her manager's abusive boss in her adulthood. So let me state this fact once more: Christians are not immune to the consequences of the curse and cultural pitfalls.

Can you see why our emotions can become a tortuous labyrinth at times? Can you understand why we need to find strategies to dissipate swelling tides of uncontrolled emotions? We can't afford to allow them to spiral out of control, causing a destructive wave that can take down loved ones as well as ourselves, similar to a tsunami that washes away everything in its destructive path.

We know when we're overreacting to stimuli. We simply don't submit it to God. It's not that Jesus cannot heal our hurting hearts. It's not a question of can He – or will He – do it. The question is *will we hand Him all the pieces?* Will we yield ourselves to the Potter's hand, and cultivate a submissive relationship to Him, first and foremost?

I am convinced that most of us end up in painful or ill-advised relationships because of some kind of warped self-image or damaged emotions – oftentimes stemming from childhood. That is why I have a thorough disgust for objectification. It is pervasive in our culture. And it causes so much damage to our psyches at an early age.

That is why I take issue with admonitions from the ill-advised who say, "You just have to get over your emotions." No, there is healing that has to take place. We cannot simply "get over" the issues. Contrary to popular belief, "getting over" our emotions is not an issue of willpower. Even some women might think, "Well, I'll just get over this someday." No, it quite probably will surface at some point in another situation or relationship if you don't receive healing. We have to have a supernatural encounter in order for true healing to commence. The last two chapters of this book will share more about the supernatural healing we need.

See, we can't just cover it over and think, "Oh, I'll be alright." We might *look* alright to others at times, but we won't *be* alright. And we'll end up taking those damaged emotions into other relationships or into other situations where our true incapacitation eventually surfaces – sometimes over things that seem trivial to others.

Just like in a labyrinth, we will go one way and hit a wall, then will have to back up, turn around, and go another way, because our emotions will trap us in certain behaviors. But when we turn around and go another way, we hit another wall and have to back up, turn around, and proceed down another path. And on and on it goes.

This reminds me of a video game I played as a young adult. I think it was called "Mind Master." The game was set in a maze, and you'd have to traverse the maze and overcome different little mind games within the labyrinth to win. If you lost the numerous mind games within the maze, you ultimately lost the entire game if time ran out on you. I recall trying to get through the maze avoiding the pesky mind games that were difficult to master and win. The same ones would trip me up every time. So I knew if I turned a corner and ran into those mind games in the corridor, my quest to win the primary game would be over! But once I learned the tricks of how to win those nuisance mind games, I could traverse the maze and win!

That's the way our lives are in our journey to wholeness, dignity, and significance. If we never learn to win the pesky mind games – in our case, to overcome the effects of the curse and cultural traps – our quest toward wholeness, dignity, and significance is pretty much over. We'll just keep running into the same obstacles and being defeated, and starting a new game on a new day wandering around the same corridors, having never made it past a base level of existence. We'll keep getting into the same kinds of relationships, experiencing the same kinds of hurts, banging our heads against the same obstacles over-and-over again in the same mazes of human relationships.

But if we allow our supernatural God to provide us with a supernatural word, and submit our entire being to His supernatural touch, He will blast through the wall of the labyrinth and free us – not from our emotions, but from the repeated *expression* and *outcomes* of spiraling and damaged emotions.

In my personal life, I have found that I can get offended quite easily and get "short" with people, if you know what I mean. I knew this was a weakness. In fact, my family has an inside joke associated with the tendency in our family. We say, "Well, I had to act like a McCormick" when we talk about any such instance of setting someone straight, so to speak. I knew the blunt emotional reaction did not reflect Jesus. But it was hard for me to bridle it.

That is, it was difficult until a blessed soul wrote about insecurity in an article or a book I read. The author of the material shared that those who are insecure constantly feel the need to prove their competence. I could see that this was true in my life, in every area! Because of being a woman, a minority, being small in stature, and just "different," I found that I was constantly trying to prove my competence, intelligence, and adequacy in whatever tasks I was involved in doing. And if any of my competencies were questioned by anyone, I would certainly convince people otherwise in short order.

The key to my deliverance was in allowing the Holy Spirit to arrest my attention about the tendency, and convict me. Then guess what? I had to understand that who, how, and why I was female, African-American, and petite – was *designed* by God for His purpose. Therefore, it was not something to be compensated for, but something to be embraced and appreciated as unique *through* Him, *in* Him, *by* Him, and *for* Him.

I learned to accept the fact that people are going to think what they want to think about me. It does not matter what people call me. What matters is what God calls me. My job is to honor my Creator in all things, at all times.

That's the power of knowing how creation, the curse, and culture have shaped me. That's the power of knowing that it is ultimately the Lord Who validates me. We have to make a conscious effort to be cognizant of the Lord's presence and purposes at all times, particularly in the heat of emotion. This knowledge will set us free!

Let's get back to the subject of female managers that I had because I have something else important to share on overcoming emotional turmoil. My other manager – the one who sought to commit suicide – provided one of the least enjoyable working experiences I'd had to that point. She lied about the job during my initial interview. After I joined the company, she undermined my expertise and held me to expectations that were unrealistic. The company's leaders finally realized the mistake of promoting her to a place of authority, and replaced her. Company officials then assigned her to a much less prestigious position. It was a demotion, and I'm sure it caused her great disappointment and shame. Ultimately, I believe her dissatisfaction over her plight contributed to her despairing of life itself, leading to her attempted suicide. She obviously could have dealt with her dejected emotions in a better way, if only she'd had a vibrant relationship with God and allowed His perspective of her to change her attitudes about herself and others.

I recall how emotionally distressing it was for me to report to her. If I caught only a glimpse of an automobile that resembled hers as I drove down a street, my stomach would immediately tighten because of the distress she had caused me on the job. My stomach trouble was an emotionally-driven reaction to my recoiling at the mere thought of her.

But God enabled me to gain insight into her damaged emotions at an office Christmas party one year. I and a few other coworkers had put on a Christmas show for the company, singing Christmas carols to bolster morale and holiday cheer among our coworkers. (This was prior to the so-called political correctness that changed "Merry Christmas" to "Happy Holidays.")

At the conclusion of the event, my manager hugged me and said, very softly, "Merry Christmas, Donna." With those words, God immediately melted my heart for the broken little girl inside of her. Her voice sounded so sweet and innocent saying those three words. Her tone was not at all reminiscent of the judgmental, disapproving tone I had regularly experienced from her during the course of my work day. God instantly instilled a compassion for her inside my heart. For the first time,

I pitied her. She was broken inside. At that instant, my thought was *she really could be a sweet person.*

Afterward, I began to pray earnestly for her healing and restoration. Then my own emotions toward her changed. Although she was reassigned before I moved on from that company, my attitude toward her mellowed over time. It progressed to the point where if I saw a car around town that resembled hers, I would try to see if it was her indeed, to honk my horn and wave. God healed my own emotions through engaging me in sincere prayer for *her.*

This is an example of how God supernaturally healed *my* emotions through prayer for the one who caused emotional pain in my life. This is why I reiterate that we must include room for the supernatural operation of God upon our hearts. We have to submit to His ways, which are higher than our ways, and submit to His thoughts, which are higher than our thoughts (Isaiah 55:9).

God works supernaturally. But He also has set aids all around us that can be as simple as relaxation techniques or favorite spots to which we can retreat in order to "get a grip." He has solutions to our emotional dilemmas because He made us. He knows what results the curse and culture have had on us, and He knows how to remedy them.

Don't endure emotionally stressful episodes without determining to get relief in some fashion. Let God help you get back on track. Maybe you can't pursue respite immediately when you face the distressing situation. But determine that you will pursue restorative measures as soon as possible, so that God can work on you to heal you. Take that time out so He can help you to control your emotions at the next opportunity for a meltdown.

Don't allow issues to fester and have the opportunity to escalate into a dilemma that might debilitate you for the rest of your life like my former managers did. Even if your condition doesn't progress to the point of a nervous breakdown, you still want to be able to function more peacefully and productively in your relationships, don't you?

It's the little episodes collected over years that result in emotional sediment. The emotional dirt gets washed into a corner of our hearts and settles there – soiled, festered, and wounded. Don't allow little crusty hurts to form a hard callus in your emotional health.

Practical activities that renew my peace take on many forms. I like to listen to inspirational music in my car and praise God in song to remind myself of His continual presence. The music helps me to keep my mind on spiritual things. I have recordings I've made of myself reading encouraging Scriptures from Psalms, Proverbs, and even the New Testament. The recordings help me not to fall into the doldrums of discouragement.

My home state is the "road rage capital of the world" – Florida. The Lord knows I needed to keep my emotions in check behind the wheel in Florida! At one period in time, I had purchased one of those furry steering wheel covers. It was so soft and soothing – like a long-haired cat's fur. I purchased the cover to protect my hands from extreme heat in the summer and frigid cold in the winter as I gripped the steering wheel during driving. But a practical tool for physical comfort provided emotional catharsis. I was amazed at the soothing effect the cover had upon my mood while driving. The soft fur spinning through my hands as I turned the steering wheel was highly therapeutic. It was just like caressing a pet's fur – it helped relieve stress.

The key for you is to find something that ministers to you on a continual basis. Find something that facilitates a more even and steady emotional release. This is preferable to experiencing outbursts of fear, anger, and sadness which arrest your peace and cause escalating states of emotional unrest over time.

Again, I reiterate – it's perfectly normal for us to cry, to long for security, to want to talk, and so on. We were made for that. We just need to comprehend that wide scale swings or spiraling mazes of emotion are not healthy or enjoyable for ourselves or for those around us.

There are numerous practical ways to deal with emotions that tend to spiral out of control and trap us in a maze of unhealthy responses. Find your special peace-generator. And don't forget the supernatural element. God is always there, and will do what only He can do, if we let Him.

Part IV *Christ: Crowning Perspective*
11 Significant Verity

**Proverbs 7:26
For she has cast down many wounded, and all who were slain by her were strong *men*.**

To commemorate the first Earth Day in 1970, Walt Kelly created a poster of his comic strip's main animal character, Pogo, surveying his much polluted home in the Okefenokee Swamp. The poster's caption read, "We have met the enemy, and he is us." The enemy is us. You've probably heard the statement, "We're our own worst enemy." I think that is an unfortunate but true statement in some instances for us as women.

What do I mean? Consider my discussion in a previous chapter concerning the things we take for granted which basically become our own snares. They might be unobjectionable when instituted among us as children, like beauty pageants. But they could entrap us in cultural expectations which become prison-like as we grow older.

Take, for instance, my discussion of objectification. Our culture is obsessed with the objectification of women. I recall attending a dance production near the year 2010. The event was organized by a local dance studio owned by a woman. The production's routines included youth of all ages, both male and female. However, I was particularly concerned by the four-year-old to five-year-old girls who were shimmying like Las Vegas showgirls, in full characteristic garb and makeup. These preschoolers were already being indoctrinated into our culture's bent on treating females as sex objects rather than as complete persons.

I believe one of the most gratifying forces in our lives is to be considered special or significant to others. It is extremely edifying to be appreciated just for who we are, inside and out. Those whom we desire to appreciate our individual significance include our children, our husbands, our employers, our siblings, and our friends. Sometimes, simply having *anyone* value our uniqueness is enough. Being valued as significant in the eyes of another is a life goal of most people. But I believe the need is more acute among women. Aside from romantic involvement, relationships *in general* are usually paramount to how we value ourselves as women.

Why is that true? Let's go back to the beginning. God created woman *in particular* for relationship. He designed us for relationship, and infused the longing within us to be in relationships, *from the beginning* of our existence. The curse concerning our "desire" for our husbands simply intensified the longing that was already present. It is very normal to desire to be significant in the life of another. We were made for that. Not that the male is not acclimated toward relationships. It's just that females are more driven by interaction among fellow humans than males are. Women are generally more socially-driven than men are.

I'm sure there aren't a great deal of sociologists or psychologists who would take issue with that statement. As women, we feel that we absolutely have to have a social dimension to our lives that makes us feel valuable. We absolutely have to have some significance in *someone's* life. It's natural, and supernatural, in fact, for our emotional health. We were designed for it.

An amusing example is a comedian's routine in which he stated that female friends dining at a restaurant will convert a simple trip to the bathroom into a social excursion. "Come go with me to the ladies room," one woman might say to her girlfriend at the table. And off they would go to the restroom together. The comedian's punch line was that two men on a lunch engagement would *never* make such a request of one another! Can you imagine such a thing? ("Hey, man, come go to the john with me.")

Generally speaking, women build *interaction into their activities*, while men tend to build activities around interests. That's because women are more relationship-driven than men. It illustrates a basic tendency that we have as women. It is reflective of our design from the beginning.

Note that I am sharing generalities here. Primarily, I'm talking about emotionally- and psychologically-balanced women, for the most part. I'm sure there are ladies dealing with very oppressive situations who tend to shun interaction with others. So I'm not generalizing about women who prefer to be reclusive due to a maladjustment to life.

Even so, many women who are living normal lives by general appearance have emotional issues that diminish their quality of life to a measurable degree. They display the typical desires and challenges common to women, in general. But it's just that some issues are more taxing to some ladies than to others.

And so we generally like to talk or socialize as an outlet for healthy emotional expression. We plan activities that foster opportunities to converse. I'm oversimplifying things a bit here, but there is truth in what I'm sharing. Men get together over activities they have in common. Women get together just to talk! Have you ever heard of a women's social? Probably. Have you ever heard of a men's social? Probably not, or rarely, if ever.

Women relish the opportunity to simply share time with family and friends. It's vital to our emotional health that we share conversation and experiences with our friends or family, so that we feel valued. This is one of the reasons why some women complain that their husbands "don't listen" to them. Listening is the key to tapping into what makes us tick (and to what ticks us off, I sometimes like to add). Therefore if no one is listening, we feel that no one is learning who we really are, what really matters to us, or what's happening in our lives. And that makes us feel less valued as individuals. It makes us feel unimportant and insignificant.

Sometimes this is revealed in how we relate to our spouses, family members, friends and other women, in general. That's why I began this chapter with a verse from Proverbs:

> *For she has cast down many wounded, and all who were slain by her were strong men.*
> *Proverbs 7:26*

This Scripture is from a passage that warns a young man of engaging with a prostitute. However, I think the verse can be universally applied to those of us who are wounded emotionally. The saying "hurt people hurt people" is very true. When wounded, we can hurt those closest to us – even our "strong" husbands, in ways that are deep and lasting. We become our own worst enemies when we begin to injure those close to us. They are the primary resources upon whom we should rely for emotional and social affirmation.

But whether or not those around us appreciate our value, we absolutely must find the value in ourselves that *God* places in us, in order to begin our journey to complete wholeness. This is where my path to God was cemented, and where I believe I can show you *your* value to God, as a woman – exclusive of your gift or calling, exclusive of your perceived attractiveness, exclusive of your intelligence, exclusive of your financial status, exclusive of the number of children you're raising or have raised, regardless of whether you have a husband or are single, regardless of whether you are divorced, regardless of whether or not you have friends, a best friend, or no friends. You have value simply because you represent God's creation, *woman*.

You see, my life is simultaneously typical and atypical of most women in our U.S. society. I am an enigma for most people to comprehend. There is very little in my life that is typical, on the *surface*, of the majority of women, worldwide. Yet my emotional, social, and psychological journey parallels the path of most women, particularly Christian women.

I love being a woman. I love God. I love God's people. I love children. I love men and the attention of a man. I'm considered to be fairly intelligent and a fun person to be around. Some might consider me to be attractive. However, I've never been married and I have no children. I have not experienced the life stages that are considered to be normal and expected for most women. Sometimes I considered them – such as getting married or having children – but many times I was glad I hadn't experienced those particular facets of life. I have been happily single for a very long time. But that doesn't mean that I have never dated or contemplated a serious relationship at various times in my life.

I believe that's precisely why God inspired me to write this book. As a woman, I'm very different, but simultaneously I am very much the same as other women. Like you, my journey began with creation, was affected by the curse, and is impacted by culture *in the same ways as yours* because we all are God's creation of "woman," in all of her unique and beautiful reflections in the earth.

I share longings of love and acceptance with you, even though my life has been very different from most of your lives. I have gained victory in the areas of wholeness, dignity, and significance, where many of you might still struggle. I can shine a different light in the dark, and perhaps show some of you the way I found my healing *outside* of relationship-based affirmation. And that is vital, because we will not find genuine significance, absolute wholeness, or legitimate dignity generated from how other people treat us. We only experience these attributes in a true and *complete* sense from our God and Creator. His love and acceptance is eternal and not predicated upon performance or meeting an arbitrary standard imposed by fallible people. Human frailties can impede our receiving affirmation from those around us, as many of us have experienced. You have friends, children, husbands, or boyfriends, and some of you have had multiple individuals in these roles. But you remain unfulfilled.

True wholeness, dignity, and significance that we long for as God's created *woman* come from God and God alone. This is a significant truth that you need to comprehend.

My struggle to obtain significance in the life of others is very typical of all of us. However, my search for significance, value, and self-esteem – qualities that many women obtain superficially from human relationships – did not have a relationship framework upon which to form in my life. There was no husband. There were no children. There were no friends with whom I shared social interaction or interests for most of my life.

Therefore I had to find my significance and value in God *alone*. Otherwise, I would have despaired even of life as so many others have done. In fact, I did. But God's grace kept me from doing harm to myself and ending it all. I wanted "out of here" because I had no other avenue of affirmation to measure my value as a human being: no friends, no children, and no mate.

So in a sense, I have an advantage that many of you might not have. God and His Word were my only sources of affirmation for significance and value as a living soul. I discovered my value in God. That's why I can tell you that regardless of who is around you, or who likes you, or who loves or doesn't love you, your significance is in the simple truth that God values you just because you're *you*.

I endured many years feeling devalued due to lack of affirmation and acceptance from those around me. I suspect that other people – although they may live in a realm full of social interaction – are also searching for significance and affirmation. The search for significance and subsequent fallout when it is not realized as hoped are possibly a contributor to statistics depicting high divorce rates, increasing suicide statistics, climbing instances of depression, increasing health issues, and even greater dissatisfaction of the populace concerning careers. We want to matter to someone. We want our lives to matter somehow. We want to be respected. We crave appreciation. We desire acknowledgement of our needs.

It's interesting to note how many people on social media share entirely too much information about their personal lives online. Have you noticed that? It seems as though they are trying to get attention, saying in essence, "Look at me. Listen to me. I matter. Does anyone care?"

The search for significance is not isolated to women exclusively, of course. However, since I am addressing the journey of women back to wholeness, dignity, and significance, let's continue with that subject matter.

The fallout from the curse and culture are not God's final perspective of *woman*. Although some people in our day would like to relegate *woman* to her fallen state, and leave her open to the ravages of culture's objectification, I submit to you that God's place for *woman* is still highly esteemed by Him.

Most of us will acknowledge that in some instances, tradition (both inside and outside of the church) has relegated women to a place of inferiority. Although some might interpret God's command to be submissive to husbands as repressive, neither God's perspective nor His intent was any such thing.

We can see God's heart concerning *woman* in several places in the New Testament. This is ironic, since the New Testament is the usual portion of the Bible, along with Genesis, which is used to make us feel like second-class citizens in the kingdom of God. I feel that I must share this because some might believe the most salient contribution of *woman* was at the fall, when she led the way to disobedience to God. Although *woman* was integral in the fall, God also utilized her in the first advent of Jesus Christ via Mary for the virgin birth. He then utilized *woman* as the first evangelist in the person of Mary Magdalene after Christ's resurrection. "Woman" was also represented in the upper room at Pentecost when God sent His Holy Spirit.

Additionally, let's take note of several places in the New Testament where women were expressly mentioned as central to the foundation of the church. Specific mention was made of women in several verses, as if God wanted us to see that we are just as important and special to Him for His entire plan as are men. This is not to bring men down, but to elevate "woman" back to God's prepared place for her. Please make note of the following Scriptures (emphasis added by me):

> *At Joppa there was a certain disciple named **Tabitha, which is translated Dorcas**. This **woman** was full of good works and charitable deeds which she did.*
>
> *Acts 9:36*

> *Some of them were persuaded and joined Paul and Silas, as did a great many of the devout Greeks and **not a few of the leading women**.*
>
> *Acts 17:4*

> *Many of them therefore believed, including **not a few Greek women and men of high standing**.*
>
> *Acts 17:12*

> *But some of them joined him and became believers, including Dionysius the Areopagite and a **woman named Damaris**, and others with them.*
>
> *Acts 17:34*

> *There he found a Jew named Aquila, a native of Pontus, who had recently come from Italy with*

> ***his wife Priscilla****, because Claudius had ordered all Jews to leave Rome. Paul went to see them...*
>
> *Acts 18:2*

These Scriptures comprise a few of the times women were specifically called out as being among those coming into the knowledge of the risen Savior. It is interesting to note that the Pauline epistles habitually mentioned Aquila and Priscilla together. Paul referred to the couple five times in his epistles. Paul mentioned Priscilla first on two occasions. I believe that is an indication of the level of esteem to which she was held by God and man. God seems to have no reservations about showing His regard for "woman."

Are you beginning to see *woman* from God's perspective now?

In our search for significance, we must be careful not to seek for it in ways that are dishonoring to God. If we don't turn to Him for the truest sense of significance, we will be driven to find it elsewhere. We can take our lesson of what *not* to do from the account of Judas.

The Bible records the fact that Judas was a thief. He was stealing from the treasury of Jesus' ministry as recorded in John 12:6. At that time, being "one of the twelve" and handling the money was Judas' route to significance. However, at some point, Judas apparently became disillusioned with Jesus and His discussions concerning His death. Judas eventually surmised that there would be no significance to his life if Jesus died, for he did not comprehend God's resurrection plan. Judas realized that there'd be no fulfillment of his ambitions for lasting significance when Jesus died. That realization ultimately caused him to betray Jesus for thirty pieces of silver. In other words, Judas betrayed a friend for money. He betrayed Jesus for *money*, which had constituted one of his perceived routes to significance in the first place.

People oftentimes search for significance by associating with someone they feel possesses significance. They want to ride the tide of someone else's significance to fame and fortune. Or minimally, they seek perks or greater self-esteem by associating with someone of significance. They want to affiliate themselves with someone who possesses popularity or fame as their own way of gaining special consideration. But if "significance by association" falls through, some people certainly will sacrifice loyalty in search of significance via someone else, money, or fame. Sometimes people even betray a friend to achieve significance, like Judas did.

Seeking significance through others is a temptation, indeed – particularly for women. How many times have we heard accounts of certain ladies seeking distinction by aspiring to be in acquaintance with specific men or amidst distinguished social circles? It's because of the prestige, honor, or perks the associations afforded them.

That's what groupies do. That's what gold diggers do. Of course, occurrences like this are not isolated to women. But such instances have been common among women.

Alternatively, some ladies try to gain significance by making others around themselves feel *insignificant*. This is a major way some people attempt to set themselves apart. They seem to say, "I'm somebody and you're not." That gives them a sense of significance. Some women feel they must belittle others to make themselves feel smarter, more successful, or more attractive. They try to compensate for their low self-esteem and feelings of insignificance by making others feel inadequate about their talents, goals, appearance, or accomplishments.

Do you see why we can indeed be our own worst enemies? To modify the Pogo poster caption, "We have seen the enemy, and *she* is us."

This is why, in some circles, it has been said that a female boss is the worst boss to have. Why? Because sometimes women feel a need to exercise authority in overbearing ways because they are attempting to compensate for inner feelings of insignificance or inadequacy. They seem to say, "Now that I have the upper hand, you're going to really feel how powerful I am!" Psychological and social scars have blemished us to the extent that when we gain authority in the upper echelons of corporate America – or the church, or the home – some of us are tempted to mishandle it. As a result, such ladies might have an argumentative or hostile posture in their dealings with others.

People like that – male or female – most likely have low self-esteem. They compensate for their own diminished levels of dignity and significance by abusing others. This is most assuredly not God's way to overcome one's feelings of low self-worth or insignificance. So let's look at God's way to regain our wholeness, dignity, and significance.

There are three pillars that form the foundation for our victory in these three areas. The first pillar of victory in our struggle is to embrace our universal purpose as "woman." This is the first foundational truth we must acknowledge. We could call it Christ's crowning perspective. *Woman* is God's vital complement for man. Our purpose and design originated from God our Creator. We were designed to help man fill the earth, to assist in governing our environment, to nurture others, and to encourage others. These tasks are to be fulfilled individually in our own families and collectively for fellow human beings in society, as well as within the house of faith.

The second foundational pillar undergirding victory in our struggle for wholeness, dignity, and significance is to recognize our physical, emotional, and relational vulnerabilities that were accentuated after the curse in Genesis chapter three. Acknowledging vulnerabilities is not an admission of failure. It is an acquiescence of awareness. Noting which specific things constitute our vulnerabilities equips us to address the deficiencies in our interactions with others. Guarding against the weaknesses helps us to protect ourselves from experiencing hurt or causing undue hurt to ourselves and to others.

For instance, if we acknowledge that we have a marked weakness for affirmation from other people in our lives, we can bolster our resolve to avoid demeaning ourselves to get such affirmation. We can search for healthier avenues to strengthen self-esteem. Or if we acknowledge our tendency to react in overpowering, controlling ways, we can be wary of the situations where such reactions would be a temptation. We can devise alternative ways beforehand to behave more amicably.

The third and final foundational pillar upholding victory in our journey to wholeness, dignity, and significance is to recognize the role of culture in perpetuating our plight. We treat cultural trappings as trivial and innocuous, when in fact they can serve to strengthen the chains that bind us. We simply do not have to go with the flow when the flow is taking our emotions into a psychological dump.

This does not mean you have to abandon things that affirm your personal femininity. But you should question or reassess some things that minimize your personhood. Refuse to be objectified, as a general principle – if not for yourselves, for the sake of your daughters or granddaughters. Impart to them their value sans any physical, social, or cultural trappings they might or might not possess. Support what others are doing to restore the self-esteem of girls and women. What good thing you do for others, God will reciprocate to you (Ephesians 6:8).

These foundational pillars are critical in helping you to achieve wholeness, dignity, and significance *without* requiring affirmation from anyone around you. We must enlist our Creator's perspective because He alone has the full picture of *woman*.

As an addendum, remember to find your secret place where you and God can be alone as you partake of emotionally-stabilizing, restorative activities *frequently*. The greatest of these activities is to earnestly pray for God's healing touch upon those who have caused emotional or psychological injury to you – past and present. Expect a healing miracle from God. Remember that He restores (refreshes) your soul (Psalm 23:3). Believe Him to do that for you.

It is no menial thing that this chapter is titled "Significant Verity." Verity is another word for truth. Jesus said, "And you shall know the truth, and the truth shall make you free" (John 8:32). Therefore, truth is critical to our restoration. God's perspective of "woman" is truth. Regardless of what others say or do – and regardless of how we think or feel – God's perspective of *woman* is the epitome of who we are, how we are, and why we exist. It is Christ's crowning perspective that sets us in the place of dignity and significance, which leads the way to wholeness.

Part IV *Christ: Crowning Perspective*
12 Supernatural Victory

John 8:11b
And Jesus said to her, "Neither do I condemn you; go and sin no more."

The account of the woman taken in adultery in John chapter eight shows a special side of God's heart toward *woman*. After making it plain that her accusers need not think more highly of themselves than they ought, Jesus never mentioned the specific sin of the woman taken in adultery. He did not judge or condemn her, even though she was caught in the very act of adultery. He simply admonished her to "go and sin no more" (John 8:11b). He gave her back her dignity. He spoke words that empowered her to take back her self-esteem. He saw in her the woman that He created, not the one she had become. His mercy spoke to the royalty within her, even though others judged her as deserving of no respect at all.

I remember when I was a college student. I was not a Christian in those days, although I recognized God's existence. During those college years, my self-esteem was probably at its lowest ebb in my entire life. However, I resided in a dormitory that housed senior and junior class honor students. One day, after a tiring day of classes, I was wearily walking down the long hallway of the dorm. I resided in a corner room at the opposite end of the building. My steps rang out with a crisp thud from the heels of my boots upon the tile floor in the hallway. I was tired, so I was walking slowly. My steps echoed in the hallway with a sharp *clop, clop, clop, clop* sound.

After I had walked about halfway down the hall, one of my dorm mates opened the door to her room and peered out into the hallway. I turned around because I heard the door open and her voice as she exclaimed, "Ah! I had to see who that was with such a stately walk."

At that time, I did not know the meaning of the word *stately*. I had to look it up in a dictionary. Stately means dignified, elegant, regal, and majestic.

Remember that I said that my self-esteem was virtually nonexistent at that stage in my life. I was in my junior or senior year of college and had no real friends on a campus of over thirty-four thousand students. Additionally, I had never had any real friends, in my estimation, up to that time. I had grown up being extremely introverted. And being a nerd with strong morals didn't help, either. So I was alone, lonely, and despondent. Yet the sound of my footsteps in a hallway seemed regal, elegant, dignified and majestic to someone else! Even to this day, I marvel at the memory of the incident.

Although my psyche and emotions were in shambles at that time, who I really *was* seeped through. And that's reminiscent of what God sees in us, because He knows what He created. His royal design for *woman* is still there, underneath all the crustiness of time and sin. The remnant of what He created seeps through. He sees the glory of His handiwork, and recognizes it, just like my dorm mate recognized a stately aura in how I walked. I might have seen myself as valueless, but my dorm mate recognized a regal, dignified elegance in the way that I carried myself. God's *woman* shined through.

We are daughters of a King. We are royalty, indeed. That's who and what we *are*. Our victory over the burdens imposed by the curse and culture requires the supernatural power of God. It is wonderful for our husbands, children, or friends to affirm us and make us feel special. But our true wholeness, dignity, and significance should originate from knowing we're special to our God. We're somebody simply because we are "woman" – His creation.

I realize that sounds simplistic. I know it sounds like a cliché. But it is the absolute truth. It is Christ's crowning perspective of us. It is the *epitome* of our significance.

Our loved ones and friends are human and fallible, just as we are. They will disappoint us, hurt our feelings, forget our birthdays, and inevitably neglect to do things that bring us happiness at some point – sometimes, more often than not. (It might seem like they take turns at it for some of you!)

But when we discover our true value to Christ Jesus, and recognize that it is His still, small voice to which we should listen, we can overcome the things that chip away at our self-worth, dignity, and sense of significance. Through looking at ourselves from Christ's viewpoint, we can gain strength to stand in spite of the things that wreck our emotions and assault our self-esteem. It is His compassion and grace toward us specifically as His creation of "woman" that paves the road to restoration. It's His grace that brings us to wholeness, dignity, and significance.

Consider another Bible passage that illustrates God's wonderful relationship with "woman." You and I have undoubtedly read or heard these Scriptures numerous times. But allow the Lord to illuminate something you might not have realized previously. This will help you to feel *God*. Let's take a look at the twentieth chapter of John, starting at verse one:

> *¹Now on the first day of the week Mary Magdalene went to the tomb early, while it was still dark, and saw that the stone had been taken away from the tomb.*
>
> *²Then she ran and came to Simon Peter, and to the other disciple, whom Jesus loved, and said to them, "They have taken away the Lord out of the tomb, and we do not know where they have laid Him."*
>
> John 20:1-2

This of course is the account of the discovery of our Lord Jesus' empty tomb. After Mary Magdalene saw that the tomb was empty, she ran, the Scripture says, to report the missing body of the Lord to the disciples.

We don't know how far Mary ran to report the shocking news of the empty tomb. But we can probably rightfully presume that she was in a panic. At that point, she did not know that Jesus had risen. She only knew that His body was missing from His place of burial.

How would you feel if you went to pay your respects to a deceased loved one only to find that the loved one's remains were nowhere to be found? For instance, if you went to a funeral and the casket was closed. But you ask them to open the casket only to see that it was empty! I'd be pretty upset. I bet you would be, too. Anyone would. The pain of losing the person in death is upsetting enough. But to discover that no one knows where the body is would greatly heighten the grief and trauma.

When the disciples and Mary arrived at the tomb, the male disciples took in the situation and left for their homes, still puzzled. So let's continue with the account of what happened next.

> ¹¹*But Mary stood outside by the tomb weeping, and as she wept she stooped down and looked into the tomb.*
>
> ¹²*And she saw two angels in white sitting, one at the head and the other at the feet, where the body of Jesus had lain.*
>
> ¹³*Then they said to her, "Woman, why are you weeping?" She said to them, "Because they have taken away my Lord, and I do not know where they have laid Him."*
>
> ¹⁴*Now when she had said this, she turned around and saw Jesus standing there, and did not know that it was Jesus.*
>
> ¹⁵*Jesus said to her, "Woman, why are you weeping? Whom are you seeking?" She, supposing Him to be the gardener, said to Him, "Sir, if you have carried Him away, tell me where you have laid Him, and I will take Him away."*
>
> ¹⁶*Jesus said to her, "Mary!" She turned and said to Him, "Rabboni!" (which is to say, Teacher).*
>
> ¹⁷*Jesus said to her, "Do not cling to Me, for I have not yet ascended to My Father; but go to My brethren and say to them, 'I am ascending*

> *to My Father and your Father, and to My God and your God.'"*
>
> *John 20:11-17*

In chapter eleven of my book, I mentioned that the Lord used "woman" as the first evangelist, to share with others the good news that He had been raised from the dead. The verses above record that commission to Mary Magdalene. The fact that she was the first person to share the good news of His resurrection constitutes a powerful commentary of the esteem with which God regards *woman*.

But that's only the beginning of what I'd like to share from this passage. The verses are rich with illumination concerning our special place as females in our Lord's heart. God knows us completely, and has made provision for the healing of His precious daughters.

Let's look deeper into the passage. In verse eleven, we see Mary Magdalene weeping at the entrance of the tomb. She is crying in distress over the horror that the Lord's body apparently has been taken. She is torn emotionally over the prospect that someone desecrated the burial spot of someone she dearly loved and wanted to honor, even in His death. Mary was absolutely devastated. Peter and John left her alone and returned to their homes. The Scriptures do not say that they sought to comfort her, or urged her to come with them. Perhaps they did, perhaps they did not. Nevertheless, she elected to remain at the tomb in her distress.

We see her remaining at the tomb, crying. She looks inside the tomb. She continues to weep. Her thoughts and emotions are no doubt spinning and raging, respectively. She's simply "being a woman" over the situation. As women, oftentimes when we're overwhelmed with emotional pain, we cry. That's what we do. That's who we are. That's how we're made. It's completely natural. It's normal. It's common. It's *us*. We are women! We sob, sometimes uncontrollably.

So at a specific point in time, Mary looked inside the tomb and saw two angels inside. They asked her, "Woman, why are you weeping?" My electronic Holman Christian Standard Bible® places a note beside the word "woman" spoken by the angels in John 20:13. The note states that for the angels to use "woman" in direct address to Mary was not a term of disrespect, but of *honor*.[8] The same note concerning use of the term woman in direct address appears in John 8:10, where Jesus began His query of the woman caught in adultery with "Woman, where are those accusers of yours? Has no one condemned you?"[9]

Returning to our discussion of Mary Magdalene at the empty tomb, the angels asked, "Woman, why are you weeping?" (John 20:13) I have a question. Do you think the angels knew Mary's name? I'm pretty sure they did. Yet they didn't call her by her name. The angels said, "Woman."

I have another question. Do you suppose angels say what they want to say, or say what God tells them to say? I believe they say what God tells them to say. In fact, I believe the reason Lucifer got into so much trouble was because he began saying things that God did *not* tell him to say, such as:

> [13]"...*I will ascend into heaven, I will exalt my throne above the stars of God; I will also sit on the mount of the congregation on the farthest sides of the north;*

> *14I will ascend above the heights of the clouds, I will be like the Most High."*
>
> *Isaiah 14:13-14*

I'm certain that God did not tell Lucifer to make those statements. That's why Lucifer was kicked out of heaven as a rebellious devil. The Lord Jesus said that He saw Satan fall as lightning from heaven (Luke 10:18). I like to say that God kicked the fire out of Lucifer. I rest my case.

So, let's get back to Mary and the angels who spoke to her. I would surmise that the angels addressed Mary Magdalene by the term "woman" because that's what God instructed them to say. Can we settle on that? Good. Let's move on.

Mary replied to the angels in verse thirteen, stating the reason for her tears – "they" (whomever she presumed them to be) had taken her Lord's body and she didn't know to where His body had been moved. So she turned away and beheld another man. She thought he was the gardener or groundskeeper, standing behind her. He also asked – get this – "Woman, why are you weeping?" (John 20:15)

Woman, why are you weeping? He used the exact words that the angels had spoken to her! But this time, those words came from the mouth of Jesus, whom Mary did not recognize. Note that the Lord, Himself, Who certainly knew Mary's name, didn't call her "Mary." He addressed her as "woman" in His first words to her. He called her "woman" just as the angels had done. He called her "woman" just like He addressed the woman caught in adultery, who the scribes and Pharisees had publicly hauled to Him.

I deduce that the salutation "woman" spoken by Jesus to Mary conferred the same degree of honor coming from Him as it did when spoken by the angels, since God was the one Who told the angels what to say in the first place. The fact that the angels used the exact words that Jesus did – *woman, why are you weeping* – supports the speculation that the Lord was honoring Mary in the same way as did the angels, by addressing her as "woman."

Hold on. There's more. I'm leading up to something.

So the Lord added, "Whom are you seeking?" And this is where Mary, mistaking the Lord for the keeper of the grounds, said something very illogical. She was totally engulfed in her emotions by this point in time. She was crying and talking *crazy*, as we might say. She responded, "... tell me where you have laid Him, and I will take Him away" (John 20:15).

Can we agree that Mary was thoroughly blinded by her emotions at this point? She was not only crying, but she didn't recognize the Lord, and was sharing that she would carry away the deceased body of a man who more-than-likely weighed more than she did. Only God knows how far.

Carry Him? Where? How? She was alone – Peter and John had left her at the tomb and gone home. She didn't even recognize Jesus – she didn't recognize Him by His voice or His appearance!

Now, we don't know if Mary's failure to recognize Jesus was due to His desire or not. However, as a woman, I'm going to share that I wouldn't be surprised if part of the reason she didn't recognize Him was because her emotions were spiraling out of control, her natural, rational mind was basically mush at that point, and her eyes were gushing over with tears. She was displaying typical female reactions that emerge when we are overwhelmed with emotions – emotions that were designed by God. But logic had left her mind. Sensibility was not in the landscape of her thoughts. She was overwhelmed with grief and shock. She was an emotional basket case, we might say.

And that's what happens to most of us, as women, in response to traumatic experiences. We cry. Our emotions get out-of-hand. Our minds oftentimes do not function rationally when we are in emotional distress as opposed to when we are not emotionally charged. That's what happens to many of us. It's normal. It's typical. We are women. That's what we do.

So imagine Mary's state. Emotions swirling. Mind overwhelmed with grief. Love for her Lord consuming her thoughts. Irrational words emerging from her mouth. And what did Jesus do?

Well, first, let's consider what He did *not* do. He did not grab her and shake some sense into her. He did not transfigure before her and say, "I AM He!" He did not command her to get out of her emotions. He did not berate her for uttering ridiculous comments. He didn't command her to stop behaving irrationally.

Mind you, this is God we're talking about – Jesus Christ, God the Son, her Lord, and *our* Lord. He did not do what many would have done in that situation.

What *did* He do? What did *He* do? He simply called her name, "Mary." That's it!

And hearing her name from the Lord caused *immediate* recognition and – get this – *instantaneous* reversal of her state of emotions! Her emotions went from one side of the pendulum to the other side, from utter devastation to full-scale elation, based on one word from the Lord. Mary's emotional state went from one extreme to the other because of one word from the Lord!

Mary exclaimed, "*Rabboni!*" And then He had to tell her not to cling to Him! I imagine Mary wanted to bear hug Him in complete joy, gladness, adoration, and love, similar to how loved ones latch on to a soldier who returns home alive from a war zone.

But notice that Mary immediately went from being completely grief-stricken and mentally anguished, to displaying ecstatic joy, in a moment's timespan. That, my sisters, is a supernatural victory. One word from the Lord, and her whole outlook changed. It's because of her relationship of complete adoration, worship, and brokenness before Him. It was due to her "forsaking all others" and due to the absolute devotion of a woman to her Lord.

Similarly, my experience with throwing the wadded slip of paper in the trash is an example of a miraculous healing from the Lord. It was a supernatural deliverance. All I did in the natural was heed the word of the Lord that came from His vessel, and responded accordingly. I wrote my affliction on the strip of paper, wadded it up, and threw it in the trash can on the altar. My healing came. That was it.

And that leads to the conclusion of this matter of *woman*. Even in the throes of what usually is our dilemma of emotion as a woman, God understands our unique constitution. Despite the framework of the curse, and despite what culture hurls at us, we still have a supernatural connection to our Lord that *He* ordained and cherishes.

He does not want us to succumb to the destructive force our emotions can become, of course. But He does not condemn us for the emotional rollercoaster on which we find ourselves on occasion in our lives. No, thank God, He does not condemn us. The Samaritan woman at the well did not encounter condemnation for her relationship troubles. Mary Magdalene did not find condemnation for her emotional meltdown. The Lord did not condemn either woman for her emotional weaknesses – He knows *woman* and how she's made!

But when He calls our name to get our attention, we need to recognize His voice. We need to listen for His still, small voice, moment-by-moment, revealing His truth to us. We recognize His voice by immersing our consciousness in His written Word, and by communing with Him in prayer at all opportunities. We foster our relationship by relying upon His sweet Holy Spirit to bring us into a captivating rapport with Him. Through this relationship, we have access to the healing balm of God.

We must recognize that it is a *supernatural* victory. The Lord desires to bring us into a place of balance concerning our emotions, and He can do that in the absence of other people around us, just as He did with Mary Magdalene. Mary was alone at the tomb, even though she had expressed her grief and dilemma to others. And for a moment, Peter and John shared in her dilemma, but then left her to deal with it alone. That's what happens to us sometimes. But the Lord Jesus did not have to utilize others to bring healing to Mary's shattered emotional state.

We cannot disregard the supernatural element of our healing because we cannot escape the supernatural element of our *being*. That is, we came into being by God's hand. "Woman" originated from a living soul into which God had already breathed His life. We continue to live and move and have our being in Him (Acts 17:28). And we will have our *well-being* in Him if we cultivate our supernatural connection to Him and nurture our love relationship with *Him*.

We focus so much on our love relationship with others in seeking affirmation and approval. But Christ's affirmation and approval is unparalleled. It cannot be matched within the frailty of human expression. We need to nurture our love relationship with *God*, first and foremost.

Thus, in conclusion, we are able to make the best out of creation, the curse, and culture by remembering the following truths as they pertain to our journey:

> *Through the Lord's mercies we are not consumed, because His compassions fail not.*
> *Lamentations 3:22*

> *"For He knows our frame; He remembers that we are dust.*
> *Psalm 103:14*

> *Nevertheless in Your great mercy You did not utterly consume them nor forsake them; for You are God, gracious and merciful.*
> *Nehemiah 9:31*

If no one but God understands your vulnerabilities and hurts, know that He is able to bring you to wholeness, dignity, and significance exclusive of the cooperation of others you look to for affirmation and love. His voice alone – in the midst of your emotional or psychological upheaval and chaos – is enough to bring healing. He knows your constitution and unique challenges as a woman – He designed you! And if all He needs to do is call your name, in the midst of your emotional roller coaster, that's all He will do to bring your healing.

He does not condemn you when your emotions have waylaid you. He is the same God today as He was at the tomb with Mary Magdalene. He has the same heart of compassion, the same mercy, and the same understanding of your unique journey as a woman. He made you! He knows.

And He's there, with you, to speak all that you need so that you can reflect the wholeness, dignity, and significance He designed into your existence – into *our* existence, individually and collectively, as His creation of "woman."

Please pray the following prayer with me:

> *Lord, I ask You to infuse my everyday existence with Your perspective of who I am, why I exist, and how I am, according to Your design for me. Please guide me to a deeper understanding of myself as Your creation. Help me to grasp my areas of weakness and lay them at Your feet. Help me not to dismiss cultural programming as trivial, but to weed out that which is detrimental to my healthy outlook about myself as Your masterpiece, "woman," the glory of man. I ask You to forgive and to heal all those who have hurt me as a result of their brokenness. I also forgive them. Please work a healing wonder in my life as I yield to Your tender touch and loving voice, in the name of Jesus. Amen.*

Welcome back, "(insert *your* name here)." *Hear Jesus speak your name as He did Mary's name at the tomb.*

Welcome back to wholeness. Welcome back to dignity. Welcome back to significance.

Welcome back, *Woman,* in Jesus' name.

ENDNOTES

Chapter 4 Advanced

[1] "advanced." Dictionary.com Unabridged. Random House, Inc. 08 Dec. 2014. <Dictionary.com http://dictionary.reference.com/browse/advanced>.

[2] Revenue of the Cosmetic Industry in the United States from 2012 to 2016 (in billion U.S. dollars), Statista.com. <http://www.statista.com/statistics/243742/revenue-of-the-cosmetic-industry-in-the-us/>

[3] "glory." Dictionary.com Unabridged. Random House, Inc. 15 Jan. 2015. <Dictionary.com http://dictionary.reference.com/browse/glory>.

Chapter 6 Perpetual Sensitivity

[4] Romance Writers of America, "Romance Industry Statistics," www.rwa.org/p/cm/ld/fid=580

Chapter 9 Low Self-Esteem

[5] McLeod, S. A. (2012). Low Self Esteem. Retrieved from http://www.simplypsychology.org/self-esteem.html.

Chapter 10 Labyrinthine Spiraling Emotions

[6] "labyrinthine." Dictionary.com Unabridged. Random House, Inc. 25 Dec. 2014. <Dictionary.com http://dictionary.reference.com/browse/labyrinthine>.

[7] "labyrinth." Dictionary.com Unabridged. Random House, Inc. 25 Dec. 2014. <Dictionary.com http://dictionary.reference.com/browse/labyrinth>.

Chapter 12 Supernatural Victory

[8] Holman Christian Standard Bible®, Copyright © 1999, 2000, 2002, 2003, 2009 by Holman Bible Publishers. Used by permission. Holman Christian Standard Bible®, Holman CSB®, and HCSB® are federally registered trademarks of Holman Bible Publishers.

[9] Holman Christian Standard Bible®, Copyright © 1999, 2000, 2002, 2003, 2009 by Holman Bible Publishers. Used by permission. Holman Christian Standard Bible®, Holman CSB®, and HCSB® are federally registered trademarks of Holman Bible Publishers.

www.ingramcontent.com/pod-product-compliance
Lightning Source LLC
Chambersburg PA
CBHW071701040426
42446CB00011B/1863